Secret
Sydney

Secret
Sydney

James Cockington

NEW
HOLLAND

First published in Australia in 1999 by
New Holland Publishers (Australia) Pty Ltd
Sydney • Auckland • London • Cape Town

14 Aquatic Drive Frenchs Forest NSW 2086 Australia
218 Lake Road, Northcote, Auckland, New Zealand
24 Nutford Place London W1H 6DQ United Kingdom
80 McKenzie Street Cape Town 8001 South Africa

National Library of Australia Cataloguing-in-Publication Data:

Cockington, James, 1952.
Secret Sydney.
Includes index.

ISBN 1 86436 317 7

1. Walking - New South Wales - Sydney - Guidebooks.
2. Sydney (N.S.W.) - Guidebooks. I. Title.

919.44104

Project Editor: Howard Gelman
Cover and Text design: Mark Thacker/Big Cat Design
Reproduction: DNL Resources
Printer: Times Offset (M) Sdn. Bhd.

Picture Credits
Fairfax Photo Library: 1, 2, 3, 7, 13, 14, 15, 19, 20, 25; James Cockington: 4, 8, 9,
10, 16, 17, 21, 23a, 23b, 24; Courtesy James Cockington: 18; Linda Marlin: 11;
Fairfax/Crawford Productions: 5; Catherine O'Leary: 22; Nicholson Museum/University
of Sydney: 26; OZ Magazine: 6; Jutta Malnic: 12

PREFACE

Sydney is not so much a city as a work-in-progress. Yet for a place that sometimes resembles a series of interconnected building sites, a surprising amount of its secret history has survived.

You have to search it out, that's all.

The monument to the sporting stadium where world history was made is hidden under the railway viaduct that replaced it. The bungalow where a comic genius died can only be seen by looking down from an elevated car park. The scene of our greatest murder mystery is a pathway only ever visited by golfers looking for lost balls.

Perhaps this is how it should be.

When you go to a new city, you tend to spend your first months seeing what everyone else sees. In the beginning, you are a tourist, even if you intend to stay forever.

Once you are settled, you enter stage two. You search out people and places that you always wanted to see, based on half-forgotten memories and vague recommendations.

The maps begin to form in your head.

The third stage is the most exciting. By now you are a part of that city's living history. You can feel its pulse. Friends point out places they would never show to a stranger. One thing leads to another. Those magic words: 'Did you know? Have you heard?'

A comment overheard in a bus leads to a story that captivates you for life. These are the secrets that only a resident can understand. You are now privy to a city's soul.

Hopefully this book will take you there.

CONTENTS

GREATER
SYDNEY

BROKEN BAY

Whale Beach

KU-RING-GAI CHASE
NATIONAL PARK

Bobbin
Head

MONA VALE

CASTLE
HILL

MANLY

Marsfield

CHATSWOOD

*PORT
JACKSON*

Lane
Cove

MT
DRUITT

North
Sydney

Westmead

Minchinbury

PARRAMATTA

SYDNEY
CBD

Prospect

Silverwater

Darlinghurst

BONDI

Auburn

Concord

Guildford

Homebush

Haberfield

Horsley
Park

Rockwood
Cemetery

Ashfield

Newtown

Kingsford

Cabramatta

BANKSTOWN

MAROUBRA

Condell
Park

ROCKDALE

Milperra

La Perouse

*BOTANY
BAY*

BOTANY BAY
NATIONAL PARK

Kurnell

Bondi Beach.

At one end = the Iceberg bar

walk along the beach to Moorish restaurant.

try the Mahi Mahi fish

or ~~Barracuda~~ barramundi

DETAIL

Freshwater

MANLY

Fairy
Bower

CHATSWOOD

Castlecrag

Northbridge

PORT
JACKSON

Lane
Cove

Cammeray

Balmoral

Mosman

Taronga
Zoo

Clifton
Gardens

Watsons
Bay

North
Sydney

Lavendar
Bay

Kirribilli

Vaucluse

Wooloomooloo

Garden
Island

Potts Point

Point
Piper

Dover
Heights

SYDNEY
CBD

Kings
Cross

Double
Bay

Rushcutters
Bay

Darlinghurst

Bellevue
Hill

Annandale

Glebe

Surry
Hills

Woollahra

BONDI

Leichardt

Camperdown

Moore
Park

Waverley

Haberfield

Ashfield

Petersham

Stanmore

Bronte

Summer
Hill

Newtown

Kensington

Clovelley

Randwick

Coogee

Kingsford

Tempe

Mascot

SYDNEY
AIRPORT

MAROUBRA

ROCKDALE

Kyeemagh

BOTANY BAY

La Perouse

ACKNOWLEDGMENTS

My thanks to the following people for advice, support
and photos during the writing of this book:
Jim Shepherd, Celeste Coucke, Stephen Fearnley,
Rocco Fazzari, Alison Gripper, Linda Marlin, Belinda Walsh
and Catherine O'Leary; with special thanks to
Kate Barnett for the loan of her bathtub in moments of stress.

walking
tours

My theory is that until you've walked a city,
you haven't really experienced it. I see these
tours as mobile history, a way to see how those
who lived here before us have shaped the city.
My choice of locations is purely personal.
Every suburb of Sydney has its own colourful
history. I hope that this book may inspire you
to explore your own favourite areas.

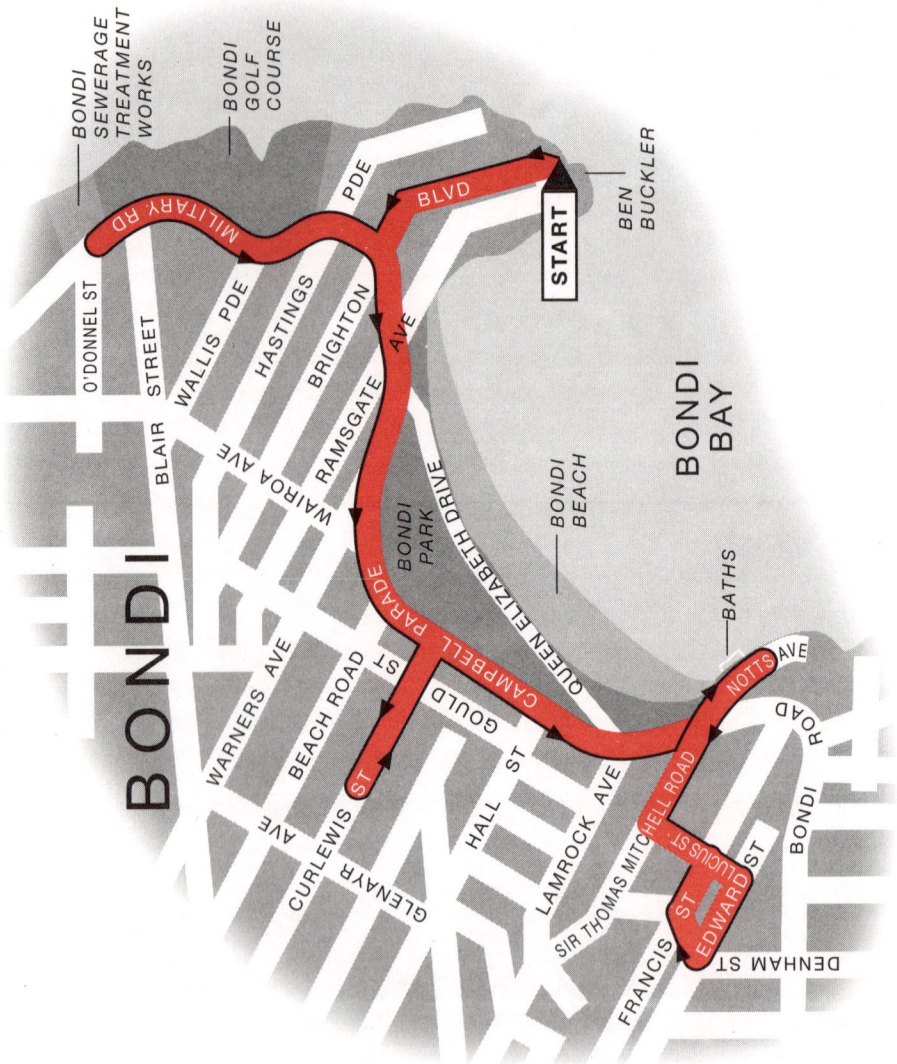

Walking

Bondi

Summary: *The most famous beach in Australia, perhaps the world, contains many secrets. Here lie some Aboriginal carvings, preserved on a rock in the middle of a golf course, while across the bay is the Icebergs Club, home of secret rituals that rival those of the Masons. And, hidden among the flats of the rich and famous, is the seedier side of life, including the sad story of the man who rode Phar Lap to victory, dying a pauper in one room of an apartment block he once owned.*

Start: *Ben Buckler, the end of Ramsgate Avenue (train to Bondi Junction, then Sydney Buses 389 or X89 to Military Road terminus, or 380 or L82 bus to Campbell Parade).*

Finish: *The Spanish flats, just behind Campbell Parade. Sydney Buses as above.*

Length: *Two kilometres.*

Time: *Two hours.*

Refreshments: *Unlimited restaurants and cafes on Campbell Parade and nearby streets.*

Bondi has been taken over by the yuppies, the backpackers and half the Australian film industry, but as recently as fifteen years ago it still had the seedy, paint-peeling charm of a seaside village, over-crowded in summer but deserted in winter.

It was a place full of characters like Jim Pike. It's one of the ironies of life that while Phar Lap has been celebrated throughout Australia—his heart in Canberra, his skin in Melbourne, his gravestone at Royal Randwick—the man who rode Phar Lap to victory died alone, broke and forgotten.

It was Jim Pike who was wearing the red and black silks when Phar Lap won the 1930 Melbourne Cup. Pike made a lot of money but had a habit of spending it soon afterwards. Like many top jockeys, he was a mug punter.

By the 1960s, he was living in a one-room dogbox in a Bondi boarding house that he once used to own. He had to sell this property, and several others he had bought in the good times, to pay off his gambling debts. Pike had a part-time job as a barman in a Bondi club but he soon lost that when decimal currency was introduced and he couldn't adapt. When he died in 1969 the police arrived to find his flat already stripped. Missing were all his old trophies and photos of Phar Lap.

That was how Bondi used to be and in some ways it still is. Beneath the froth of the cappuccino and the layers of suntan oil is a world of the hustler and the crim. The suburb that witnessed Australia's first kidnapping attempt (eight-year-old Grahame Thorne in 1960) and its first car-bombing (brothel owner Joe Borg in 1968) still has an undercurrent of violence. It's as if the more recent series of shootings, abductions and knife attacks are all part of a Bondi tradition. But hidden among the suntan freaks and the coffee shops are glimpses of its former beauty. To many, two golden mermaids are still the symbol of the suburb.

BIG BEN

In July 1912, an immense rock weighing 235 tons was washed up onto the shelf at Ben Buckler, the northern point of Australia's most famous beach. They call this rock Big Ben. In 1960, an eccentric sculptor named Lyall Randolph (the popular press dubbed him the 'Leonardo da Vinci of Bondi') designed two mermaids which sat on top of Big Ben in glamour girl poses.

The mermaids were modelled from life. Randolph's subjects were two local girls: Jan Carmody, Miss Australian Surf 1959; and Lyn Whillier, a Commonwealth Games swimmer and daughter of Evelyn de Lacy, the 1936 Olympian. The statues were cast in fibreglass and cement and painted gold.

When Jan and Lyn first appeared topless on the rock, the Catholic Church immediately wanted them removed, claiming that they would inspire young men to commit sex offences. Twenty years later, other Christian groups protested when real-life mermaids started to sunbathe topless on Bondi Beach.

The big rock looks as if it's here to stay, but the mermaids have long gone, although they have since entered the realms of Bondi mythology. One was swept off the rock in a storm in 1974 while the other, minus some body parts and a lot of gold paint, was removed before it too disappeared.

Like some crumbling archeological treasure, the remains of the second mermaid sit quietly in a back room of the Waverley Library. There have been several attempts to resurrect the mermaids, most recently by an artist called Lizmania. She wanted $500,000 to reproduce the original statues in bronze. Big Ben is still vacant.

BONDI GOLF COURSE

But any tour of Bondi should begin with the mythology of a previous culture. On a rock outcrop in the middle of Bondi Golf Course are some Aboriginal carvings, a sign that this was a happening place before white settlers arrived. Best to ask for directions from the clubhouse, which is on Military Road, just north of Campbell Parade.

Also on the golf course is the notorious stink pipe, the chimney which marks the presence of the nearby Bondi Sewerage Treatment Works. This is where most of the city's waste is collected and, until a deep water outfall system was installed in 1991, the by-products of the treatment works were unceremoniously dumped in the water, just north of Australia's most populated beach. When the tides were right, a large brown stain appeared just off Ben Buckler and was slowly washed into shore. Severe beach pollution in the 1980s inspired the famous 'Turn back the Tide' protest at Bondi in 1989. The water is clear now but locals well remember the days when swimming at Bondi was like bathing in chunky mud. Guided tours of the Bondi Treatment Works are available and are surprisingly popular.

BLACK SUNDAY

A walk along the kilometre of Bondi sand should begin with a history lesson. This is a beach that can bite back. The most famous surf disaster was on February 6 1938. They call it Black Sunday.

It was a beautiful day beneath the stately Norfolk pines that, in those days, formed a cool green backdrop. The beach was packed and the water was full of swimmers. Suddenly, the water became unnaturally still. A set of three monster waves was visible on the horizon, becoming even larger as they crashed in to shore. At least 300 people were caught in the massive rip that followed, and swept out to sea.

The lifesavers ran to the rescue but were clearly outnumbered.

'It was mass hysteria at its worst,' said Carl Jepperson, the then captain of the Bondi Lifesaving Club. 'In frenzy, they shouted, screamed, cried, begged and prayed. They grabbed, clawed and fought while some calmer surfers tried to reassure and help them.'

At one stage there were forty bodies on the sand, some dead, some unconscious. It was more like a war zone than a Sunday at the beach. In the end Black Sunday claimed only five lives. At least three victims thought to be dead were brought back to life by lifesavers. The saddest fatality was that of Carl Saur, who swam out to rescue a girl who could hardly swim. He saved her life but was himself sucked under the surface and drowned.

There has been nothing to match Black Sunday but each summer lifesavers have to rescue swimmers who get caught in the lethal Bondi rips. Most have broken the cardinal rule and swum outside the red and yellow flags.

GELIGNITE JACK

A slight detour from the beachfront takes you down Curlewis Street, just off Campbell Parade, to the Bondi Garage at No. 92. To some this is a shrine. The building once housed the business of one of Bondi's true legends, 'Gelignite' Jack Murray.

In the 1950s, Gelignite was the star of a series of round-Australia car races called the Redex Trails. These events started in the car park next to the Bondi Pavilion, just a few hundred metres from the Bondi Garage. The start alone attracted thousands of spectators. Jack Murray won the 1954 trial in a battered 1947 Ford sedan known as The Grey Ghost, and became a national hero.

The nickname Gelignite came from Murray's love of practical jokes. During the trials, he carried an ample supply of gelignite sticks which he would detonate when things got a bit boring. Country dunnies were always a popular target. Jack Murray was a devout thrillseeker. In his life he was a wrestler, boxer, pilot, waterskier, stock car racer and crocodile hunter. Above all, he was a larrikin.

'I went to see Jack Murray at Bondi,' writes Evan Green in his book, *Journeys with Gelignite Jack.* 'The garage is a long, barn-like building, flush with the footpath. A couple of kerbside petrol pumps are used to re-fuel the cabs. No other business is encouraged.'

Green recalled that, on that day in the mid-1960s, the garage was filled with two speed boats, a wrecked helicopter, a collection of waterskis and a collapsible canoe. On the walls were displayed the jaws of a tiger shark, the skull of a steer with an ingrown horn, two elephant tusks, the head of a crocodile and a fin from the biggest hammerhead shark ever caught in Australia. There were also a few human skulls. These were about the only ones not personally captured by Murray.

Taking pride of place was the 1960 Olympic flag stolen by Dawn Fraser and others during the Tokyo Olympics.

Today, Gelignite Jack's garage is owned by a relative and is run on more conventional lines. The walls are devoid of animal and human skulls, but the old Grey Ghost (recently restored) is occasionally parked outside.

BONDI'S CELEBRITIES

Likewise, today's Bondi characters are more conventional, and much wealthier. Kerry Packer's son Jamie moved in to build on a former petrol station site on the corner of Campbell Parade and Sir Thomas Mitchell Road. A block away, Jason Donovan has a flat on the corner of Lamrock Avenue.

Local residents studiously ignore the presence of celebrities in their midst. During the period when Jason Donovan made a habit of falling down in public—you can sit on the same stool he fell off at Gusto in Hall Street—the footpath outside his entrance was packed with paparazzi. But as soon as the fuss was over, Jase could still walk down to buy milk without anyone noticing. In Bondi, everyone is a celebrity, or thinks they are.

There are few constants in ever-changing Bondi, but Bates Milk Bar is one of them. This classic Australian milk bar on the corner of Hall Street and Campbell Parade has been run by the same family since the early 1960s. It retains much of the flavour of that period. The magnificent etched mirrors depicting beach scenes are original fixtures. The rear section including booths is also authentic, although few people seem to use this space. Part of the Bondi ethos is to sit where you can be seen, and this back room has no windows.

Positioned on the busiest corner of Bondi, the owners have so far resisted all temptation to sell to the highest bidder. This is good news for locals who say that when Bates goes, so do they. They say the true spirit of Bondi lives here.

BONDI ICEBERGS

Another spiritual institution lies due south of Bates, along Campbell Parade past the former Hotel Astra (where a then struggling actor named Peter Finch once worked as a waiter) and across the road at Notts Avenue. As you walk past, spare a thought for the sole surviving Norfolk pine on the beachfront park. This area was once covered with such trees, but a combination of salt damp and pollution have killed all but one. And this one doesn't look that well. More pines have been planted but it will take some time before they grow to this size. Towards the end of Notts Avenue is the yellow Bondi Icebergs Club with its seawater pool down the steps at water level. The most famous winter swimming club in the world began in 1929 with about a dozen participants. In 1960, the old clubhouse was replaced by the current premises which include a licensed club.

Strict rules apply for membership. It takes five years to become fully-fledged and during that period you have to swim three Sundays out of four, regardless of the weather or the water temperature, which can get as low as twelve degrees. To become an Iceberg takes dedication.

It is a club with rituals that some may find strange. At the opening of the winter season (when the water can still be a touch warm for their taste), the members jump in holding blocks of ice. The club president watches proceedings from a throne made of ice. When a member dies, his ashes may be scattered in the sea off the pool while fellow Icebergs line up along the edge, wearing the club's official ice-blue Speedos.

Club members range from teenagers to ninety-year-olds, from high court judges to garbos. One senior member walks with the aid of crutches but swims, every day, like a fish.

For over sixty years, the Icebergs, was strictly a men-only zone until public pressure forced the club to accept females for the 1994 season. Most agree this has been a good move.

The main social activity, apart from winter swimming, appears to be drinking, which is a year-round sport. Most of this takes place in the upstairs clubrooms which are open to the public. When it isn't too crowded, the Icebergs Club is about the best place for a drink in Sydney.

Perhaps the most famous Iceberg of all is actor Bill Hunter. There is a chair upstairs which is known as 'Bill's chair'.

The Icebergs pool, complete with stones painted to look like icebergs, is also open to the public except on winter weekend mornings. A feature of the pool is the low sea wall which allows waves to crash over in rough weather. According to legend, at least one shark has been washed into the pool while (not on the same day) a woman swimmer has been washed out.

Notts Avenue leads to one of the best known cliff walks in Sydney— past Tamarama Beach and on to Bronte. There is usually a stream of joggers and power walkers, but for those interested in Sydney's secrets, there's a slight detour back to Sir Thomas Mitchell Road, past the Packer Palace. Incidentally, the laneway to the right, just after the strangely triangular block of flats known as Sir Thomas Mitchell Mansions, is the alley where they found Martin Sharp's stolen paintings in August 1998.

Though not as dramatic as Melbourne's stolen Picasso story (one of his million-dollar paintings was stolen then left in a railway station locker), one of the missing paintings was worth at least $20,000. After fifteen months, the thieves realised the art was too easily identified to be sold so they deposited the paintings in an unlocked garage in Lamrock Lane. A note was kindly delivered to Martin Sharp who recovered his work.

THE SPANISH FLATS

If you turn next left at Lucius Street, you will see, at the next corner, the first of several Spanish mission-style apartment buildings in the block bordered by Edward and Francis Streets. Each building has a Spanish name, so don't be surprised if you start humming, 'Do You Know The Way To San Jose?' There are Santa Fe, Santa Lucia, Pasadena, Santa Cruz and Santa Barbara, but San Quentin doesn't rate a mention.

Examples of this Hollywood-inspired 1930s architectural style are scattered throughout Sydney but nowhere else to this intensity. In this solid block of Spanish missionism, there are only a few Anglo-Saxon intruders.

Waverley Library was unable to tell me whether this suburb within a suburb was the work of one builder or an example of collective inspiration. Perhaps it's better left as one of Bondi's few remaining mysteries.

WALKING
CASTLECRAG

SUMMARY: *This is a circular walk around Castlecrag, a maze-like Sydney suburb designed by Walter Burley Griffin and his wife Marion, passing by several houses designed by Griffin, including his own residence. Opportunities arise en route to see the magnificent natural beauty that inspired the designers. Also visited is the memorial to beloved actor Leonard Teale, perhaps Castlecrag's best-known resident and, on the water's edge at the boatsheds, the scene of a bizarre tragedy.*

START AND FINISH: *The Griffin Centre Shopping Complex, corner of Edinburgh Road and Eastern Valley Way. (Sydney Buses 205–208 and 266–267, buses 203 and 275 take passengers to the end of Edinburgh Road. No train or ferry access.)*

LENGTH: *Three kilometres, including some steep hills.*

TIME: *Three hours.*

REFRESHMENTS: *Shops and cafes at the Griffin Centre.*

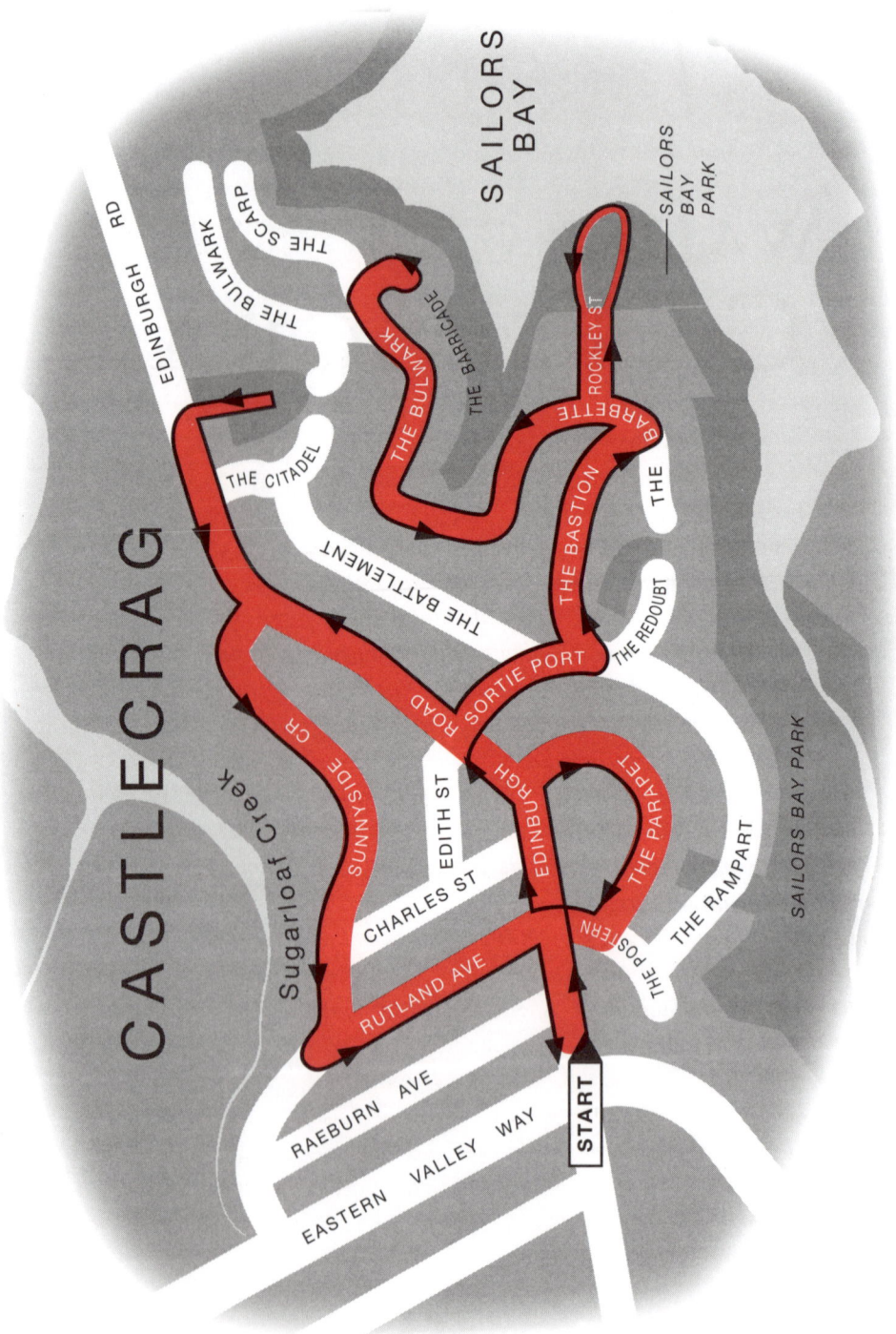

Castlecrag is to Burley Griffin what Disneyland is to that other American called Walter. Although best known for designing Canberra, this secluded Sydney suburb just north of the harbour was Walter Burley Griffin's pet project. And it was in Castlecrag, not Canberra, where he chose to live between 1924 and 1937.

American-born, Walter Burley Griffin was an early associate of Frank Lloyd Wright in Chicago, as was his wife Marion Mahony. She was also a talented architect (the first woman in the world to gain accreditation) and illustrator. Much of what the Griffins designed and built they did so in partnership. This then was their mutual dream.

By the time they came to Australia and started to design Castlecrag in 1921, both were becoming influenced by the anthroposophical writings of Rudolf Steiner. The Steiner influence is strongly evident in their work.

'Buildings are the most subtle, accurate and enduring records of life— hence their problems are the problems of life and not problems of form,' Walter Burley Griffin wrote in his essay, 'Building for Nature'.

He was given a startling piece of nature upon which to build. Approximately one square mile in area, the subdivision was noted for its rocks, trees and hills. It was surrounded on three sides by water. The Griffin ideal was to retain as much of this natural beauty as possible. Most of the original houses are built from stone quarried at the site. As well as keeping as much virgin bush as possible, he had a thousand native trees planted.

'I want Castlecrag to be built so that each individual can feel that the whole of the landscape is his,' he declared at the start of the project. 'No fences, no boundaries, no red roofs to spoil the Australian landscape; these are some of the features that will distinguish Castlecrag.'

The site had originally been called Edinburgh Castle after a unique rock formation that still (but only just) survives. Griffin, fascinated by the Middle Ages, decided to retain this medieval theme by naming many of the streets— The Bastion, The Citadel, The Parapet and others—after parts of a castle. In a sense, this was to become a kind of anthroposophical theme park.

Nice idea, but by the time he left in 1937 he had only been commissioned to design twenty local houses and, of these, only sixteen were built. While fourteen remain, some have been modified.

Like many visionaries before and since, he was a victim of bureaucracy. He had planned a suburb of low-cost, experimental housing for artists and craftspeople, but in the midst of a depression the banks refused to give home loans to bohemians.

Ironically, Castlecrag has since become a very exclusive suburb. Most of the houses built since the Griffins left for India are in the red-roof style that he hated so much.

Today, a typical home listed in the local real estate office is worth $750,000. A four-bedroom 'executive residence' is available for rent at $1,700 per week. The only artists who can afford to live here are those who are married to surgeons or television executives.

Although Castlecrag is still seen as Griffin's grand vision, there is little evidence of him today. There's a memorial plaque, but it's hidden in a small patch of bush. A more recent tribute is a brass statue of Griffin, by Judith Englert-Shead, in front of the Griffin Centre, the main shopping complex in Edinburgh Road.

A word of warning for those planning to do this walk through Castlecrag. The streets here make a reasonable impression of a maze. Initially, Griffin planned public walkways between each allotment so that shortcuts could be taken from street to street. Most seem to have disappeared, replaced by the fences that Griffin insisted had no place in his personal utopia. Walking here is a real challenge. Take a map with you because sometimes even the residents appear to be lost.

WALTER BURLEY GRIFFIN'S HOUSE

The walk starts at the new Griffin statue on Edinburgh Road, just after the intersection with the busy Eastern Valley Way that marks the main entrance to the suburb. When you walk east along Edinburgh Road, the first two of the few surviving houses designed by Walter Burley Griffin are on your right, at Nos. 136 and 140. These mini-sandstone castles are typical of the intended style, with flat roofs (so that everyone can share the view) and natural surroundings. The gardens are probably neater than Griffin intended.

These and the other original houses are occasionally open for inspection on special heritage days. The local library will have details.

The most intense cluster of Griffin houses is to be found if you turn next right at The Parapet. No. 8 is most famous. This is where Walter and Marion lived for their thirteen years in Castlecrag, although No. 12, another Griffin creation close by, is by far the more spectacular design. Note the wonderful wrought iron gate. Nos. 4 and 14 are also Griffin's.

While local stone is the most obvious building material, Griffin also used his patented Knitlock concrete blocks to construct parts of these buildings.

The Parapet forms a loop, so if you find yourself back where you started (where the statue of Griffin may now appear to be smiling at you) don't be surprised. There's a lot of circular walking to be done at Castlecrag.

Eastwards along Edinburgh Road is the corner of Sortie Port where the Community Hospital is situated. It wasn't built by Griffin but by an early resident, Dr Rivett, who faithfully followed the medieval theme. This must be one of the few hospitals in the world designed to look like a castle. On this corner, in front of the island that divides the road, is the aforementioned statue of Griffin.

Sortie Port leads us down towards the water. Take the Bastion, second left, and you'll pass by Camelot, another spectacular mini-castle, at No. 3.

SAILORS BAY PARK

Turn left then right into Rockley Street to arrive at Sailors Bay Park, one of several small nature reserves dotted throughout the suburb. This is a sacred site.

Leonard Teale, the actor best known for his role of Sergeant Mackay in the classic TV series, 'Homicide', was Castlecrag's best known resident. He died in 1994. While there have been no sightings of a ghostly figure wearing a pork pie hat ordering people to help him in his investigations, his spirit is still very much in evidence. A plaque is mounted on a rock here, where Teale liked to sit and look out over Middle Harbour.

The plaque features a quote from Robert Louis Stevenson: 'If a man loves the labour of his trade apart from any question of success or fame, the gods have called him.'

It's a fitting tribute to a much loved actor—'a real sweetie' according to fellow Crawford Productions star Michael Pate. When I last visited, the rock was adorned with a freshly picked twig of wattle. As a proud Australian who recorded several albums of bush ballads, Teale would have appreciated that.

Thanks to television exposure, Teale is probably better known than the man who actually designed the place. Other celebrities have lived here, notably rock and roller Johnny O'Keefe, but none have memorials that I could find.

SCENE OF A TRAGEDY

These pockets of native bushland are like jewels in an increasingly car-ravaged suburb, but this one has a sad story to tell. Just to the left of Leonard Teale's memorial is a one-lane pathway leading down through the reserve to the Mowbray Point boatsheds. Down is an understatement. The road practically drops off the cliff. This notoriously steep lane figured in Castlecrag's most tragic event.

Australia Day, 1963, was a typically hot and humid Sydney summer's day. A motor cruiser was anchored in Sugarloaf Bay, the secluded inlet that marks the northern edge of Castlecrag. Two of the six on board were Marcia Hathaway, a thirty-two-year-old actress, and her fiancé, Frederick Knight. They had swum to the rocky shore to cool down and look for oysters. Marcia was up to her hips in the water when she screamed out, 'I've been bitten by an octopus!'

In fact, it was a shark, later to be identified as a bronze whaler. Knight tried to grab his fiancée but the shark was determined. Its jaws were locked around her foot. With the help of another friend, they freed her mutilated leg.

Back on board, her friends ripped up sheets and applied tourniquets. Marcia Hathaway was in deep shock. Even so, she was able to describe what the inside of a shark's mouth feels like—soft and spongy.

Sugarloaf Bay, as you will see for yourself if you look out off the reserve at Sunnyside Crescent, is enclosed by near-vertical cliffs. There's no way up or down. The closest point to civilisation is south, around Sugarloaf Point, and across to the boathouses at Mowbray Point. It must have been an agonisingly long journey for help.

Passing the waterfront homes at Cheyne Walk, a desperate Fred Knight dived off and swam to the nearest house, phoning for an ambulance. They were relieved to find an ambulance waiting for them when the boat arrived at the boatsheds. Thanks to the clear, calm actions of her friends, it now seemed likely that Marcia Hathaway would survive this ordeal.

But the second stage of this tragedy was about to begin, at the bottom of this steep slope. With Marcia in the back, the wheels of the ambulance failed to grip on the slippery surface. The air was filled with tyre smoke and the acrid smell of a burnt clutch. To everyone's horror, the ambulance was unable to climb back up the hill.

'An incredible scene followed,' writes Alan Sharpe in his book *Shark Down Under.* 'Thirty able-bodied men closed in around the vehicle and with every ounce of muscle, heaved and strained to push it up the hill. The heavy ambulance refused to move.'

Another ambulance had to be called. Sensibly, it waited at the crest of the hill while Marcia Hathaway was transferred to it. By the time she made it to Mater Misericordiae hospital, she was dead.

To try and struggle up the hill now, even on foot, is to realise how futile it must have been then. And now, unlike then, the road is smoothly sealed.

It's worth noting that when Griffin designed Castlecrag, one of his original plans was to keep sharks out of Middle Harbour with a system of nets. It was seen as a ludicrous idea and the scheme was shelved.

THE MOWBRAY POINT BOATSHED

Despite its tragic history (and the daunting prospect of a trip back up the hill) the boatsheds at Mowbray Point are well worth visiting. A small track takes you behind the toilet block and the boatsheds to a series of neat steps carved out of one large boulder. The steps take you down past the Greig Charnell memorial boatshed (dedicated to a former Sea Scouts leader who lost his life in South America) to a natural bay surrounded by rocks where it is easy to forget that you are only twenty minutes from the CBD. There are even mangroves growing here.

But those with memories stretching back to 1963 will soon tell you this is no place for a swim, or even paddling. The tragic story of Marcia Hathaway reflects the overall impression of today's Castlecrag as being difficult to access. There are too many cars and not enough road. When Walter Burley Griffin designed this suburb, he was thinking about people and nature, not automobiles. Back in 1921, even this visionary architect couldn't have foreseen the day when every house here would have at least two cars, plus a constant flow of service vehicles (renovations!) throughout the day.

At times, traffic is as much a problem here as it is in George Street. With not enough room to park cars in the street, residents have gone to extraordinary lengths to squeeze garages onto their blocks. Some, propped up on stilts, are probably worth a complete house out Penrith way.

Pedestrians should be aware of this as they walk the narrow streets, some of which are too narrow for footpaths. Avoiding passing traffic takes much of the pleasure out of visiting here.

The next stage of the Griffin tour is back up Rockley Street. Turn right where it meets The Bulwark. This street (one of the narrower ones, and without footpaths) winds along the cliff until, just after intersecting with The Scarp, you'll find a turnoff to a cul-de-sac called The Barricade.

THE AMPHITHEATRE

On this corner, hidden among the trees, is perhaps Walter Burley Griffin's greatest work. This is the amphitheatre, the sole survivor of many planned community projects for Castlecrag. It is an open-air theatre created from a natural hollow, with rows of sandstone steps for seats and a creek, literally, running underneath the stage. A tree pokes up through a hole in the stage.

The amphitheatre is still used occasionally for local performances but this venue is rarely promoted and doesn't even appear to be signposted. Even without attending a performance, a trip to this theatre is an inspiration. During the latter days of his Castlecrag period, this was Griffin's favourite place. Much of it was built with his own hands.

There is a small memorial here among the tree ferns: 'Judy Bowen loved this amphitheatre, 1947–1989.' It's easy to see that she wasn't the only one.

For another dose of Griffin magic, it's back the way we came (unless you can find a shortcut that I couldn't) and up the hill to Edinburgh Road. Walking further east takes you past several more interesting houses, including one with a dolphin sculpture on the rock at No. 187, and the one with the white turret at No. 215.

THE CITADEL

It is worth a quick detour down the street known as The Citadel to see what is regarded as the best of the original Griffin houses, the Fishwick castle at No. 15. A grander home than the one Griffin himself chose to live in, it originally featured two fishtanks set in the dining room ceiling. The current owner, Andrew Kirk, discussed the joys and frustrations of living in an original Griffin in a video produced for the Powerhouse Museum's 'Beyond Architecture' exhibition.

'They almost all leak' admits Kirk. 'You have to be both a cretin and have very deep pockets to enjoy living in a Griffin house.' He added that these places are almost impossible to decorate. 'You can't superimpose your personality on it.' He did say it was a great privilege to live where he does. This block of land is pie-shaped so the best views are from the back. One of the bedrooms has windows with 180-degree views over the harbour. Worth putting up with some leaks for that.

Walking back to Edinburgh Road, and just past the turnoff to The Citadel is a signposted laneway to Tower Reserve. On the right as you walk down this lane is an outcrop of rocks which, I suspect, may be the ones that gave this area its original name of Edinburgh Castle.

It's not easy to get to the top of the rocks (and these days some of the adjacent back gardens appear to have claimed some of this territory), but if you can get up you will be rewarded with the best views in the district. This appears to be the highest point of Castlecrag. From here you can see the city and the sea.

CRAG COVE

Equally breathtaking views are to be found closer to the beginning of the walk. If you head back down Edinburgh Road and turn right into Sunnyside Crescent, there is a small park between the first group of houses which overlooks Crag Cove and Sugarloaf Creek.

This is a wilderness ravine worthy of the Blue Mountains and must be what inspired Walter Burley Griffin when he was first shown this site. There's a rock here carved into the shape of a lounge chair if you want to sit and meditate for a while. This is the magic of Castlecrag. Just fifty metres off the main street is a view you would normally have to drive more than fifty kilometres to enjoy.

Any of the roads turning left off Sunnyside Crescent will return you to Edinburgh Road. From there it's a short walk back to the starting point. A choice of cafes awaits you at the shopping centre, as does another Castle-crag treasure, the charming old-fashioned butcher shop (sorry, make that purveyor of meats) on the corner of Raeburn Avenue. Cured hams are the speciality. They proudly advertise the fact that they won first prize for these at the 1994 Royal Easter Show.

WALKING

GARDEN

ISLAND

SUMMARY: *This is a guided tour that is normally off-limits to civilians, with a naval history dating back to the first white settlement. You can see the enormous Graving Dock facility built for World War II, and the site of the 1942 HMAS* Kuttabul *disaster, when Japanese midget subs fired on Sydney Harbour. Also, Australia's first example of graffiti and, subject to availability, the haunting Clarens Gardens, the remains of a nineteenth-century Grecian-style paradise just a few hundred metres from Kings Cross can be seen. For details of the Garden Island tour, phone 02 9359 2371. There is no fee but a small donation is welcome.*
START: *Corner Cowper Wharf Roadway and Wylde Street, Potts Point (Sydney Bus 311. No ferry service at present, although a service is planned in time for the 2000 Olympics).*
FINISH: *Wylde Street, opposite corner of Grantham Street (Sydney Bus 311, nearest train station is Kings Cross on the Bondi Junction line).*
LENGTH: *Two kilometres, includes one relatively steep hill.*
TIME: *Two hours (another half hour if Clarens Gardens is accessible).*
REFRESHMENTS: *Pubs with good food at Woolloomooloo, one kilometre away down Cowper Wharf Roadway, or a choice of cafes and milk bars, two hundred metres along Macleay Street.*

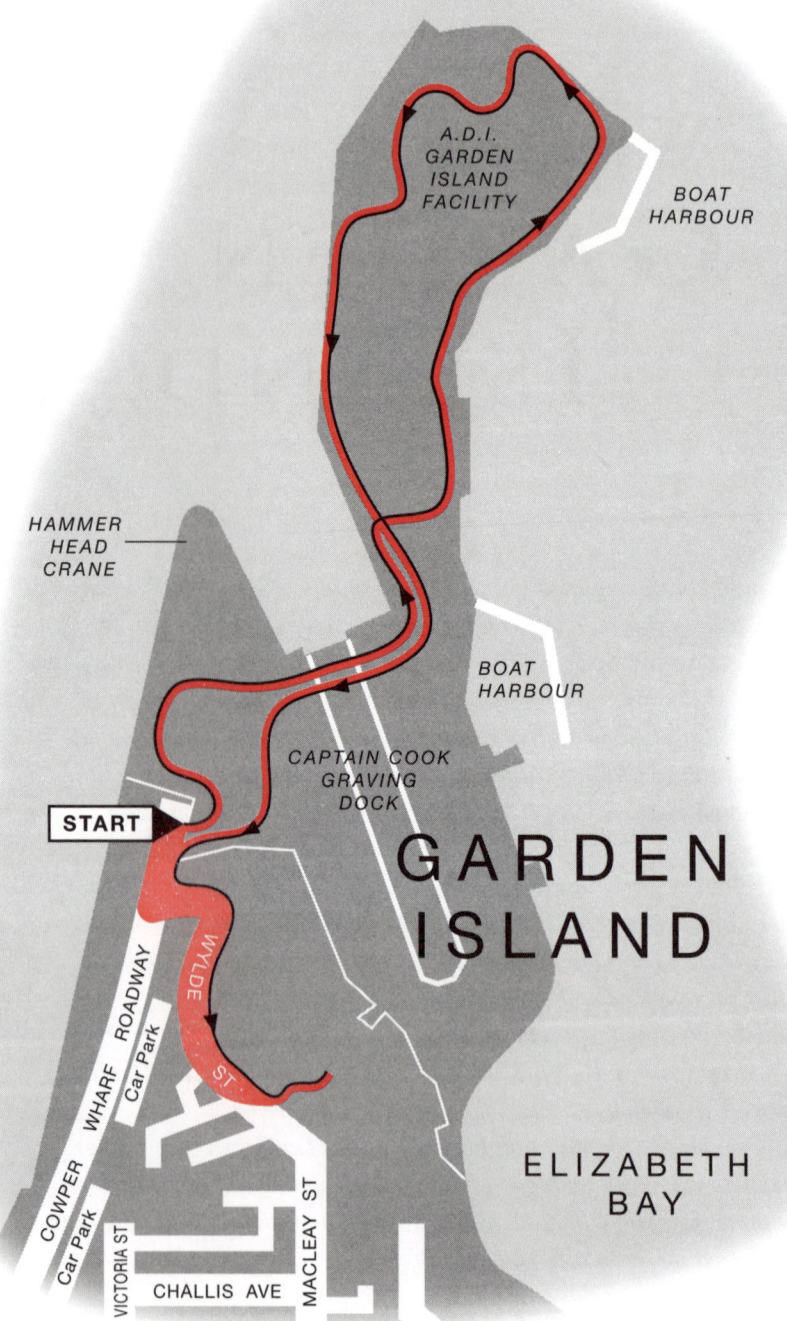

PORT JACKSON

A.D.I.
GARDEN
ISLAND
FACILITY

BOAT
HARBOUR

HAMMER
HEAD
CRANE

BOAT
HARBOUR

CAPTAIN COOK
GRAVING
DOCK

START

GARDEN
ISLAND

ELIZABETH
BAY

WYLDE ST

COWPER WHARF ROADWAY

Car Park

Car Park

VICTORIA ST

CHALLIS AVE

MACLEAY ST

You can't get much more secret than Garden Island. This mini-suburb just down the hill from Kings Cross is normally restricted to Navy personnel, so we civilians are forbidden. But on most Tuesdays and Thursdays, guided tours of this historic site are conducted at 10am. It's a rare chance for outsiders to see what goes on here.

First, it should be explained why this so-called island is only partially surrounded by water. In the 1930s, when the threat of war was looming, it was decided to turn the facility into a modern naval base, complete with a dry dock. This involved reclaiming much of what used to be under water and connecting the island to the mainland. In fact, as will be graphically pointed out on the tour, the original area of island is now a relatively small part of the entire site.

Garden Island was first called Saddle Island by the crew of HMS *Sirius* in 1788. Apparently its silhouette resembled a saddle from a distance. But when Governor Phillip decided to use this site to grow vegetables (mainly onions and corn) it became better known as Garden Island, and the name stuck.

Its potential as a prime location for naval supplies and repairs was soon realised, and by the late nineteenth century, stone buildings, some three storeys high, had replaced the vege patch. Fortunately many of these historic structures still remain on the original island section, and even better, most are now being restored with historical accuracy.There are plans to fence off this historic section so that visitors can have freer access without having to go through the security gates at the bottom of Wylde Street. If this happens, visitor access is likely to be by ferry and Garden Island will certainly become one of Sydney's more interesting tourist destinations.

CAPTAIN COOK GRAVING DOCK

As the tour stands at the moment, first stop is the dry dock facility, the reason for Garden Island coming into its present state during World War II. Officially known as the Captain Cook Graving Dock, this astonishing piece of engineering is 350 metres long, nearly fifty metres wide and (reverting to the imperial measures printed on the sides) forty-five feet deep. Any ship that will fit into this theoretical box is floated in, then the water pumped out (this can take up to four hours) leaving the ship high and dry.

Another feature of this section of Garden Island is the hammer-head crane built in 1941. Apart from a temporary crane used in the construction of the 2000 Olympics complex at Homebush, this veteran is still capable of lifting heavier weights than any other crane in Australia. You don't have to be in Garden Island to see this crane, of course; it is visible from just about any city skyscraper, and from aircraft. But this relatively modern use of Garden Island is not what most people come to see. A hundred metres from the dry dock is an imaginary line that marks the edge of the original island. Step over this line and you step back a century and a bit.

The Rigging Shed, built in 1887, was formerly used as a sail loft. Now, part of the upstairs space is used as the Naval Chapel. The interior is fitted out with former ships' timbers (the lectern is shaped like the prow of a boat) and the many stained glass windows, dedicated to former ships and their crew lost in action, have all been supplied by Navy personnel. Some of these windows are priceless works of art.

The interior of the main chapel includes an elevated section along one wall which was traditionally occupied by prisoners. At one stage, this space had to be enclosed with wire mesh to prevent the prisoners from throwing objects at the officers sitting below. Corners of the pages of the Bible, chewed into spitballs, were the most popular missiles.

Next to the chapel is the Barracks, built in 1888. This is a three-storey building built in the colonial style to accommodate up to 254 Royal Marines (who slept in hammocks, of course). The top floor was formerly a hospital. More recently, two wooden figureheads have been placed in front of the verandas. One, from the yacht the *Windsor Castle*, is of Queen Victoria, showing how she looked in 1876. The other figurehead is of Consuela Vanderbilt, of the very wealthy American dynasty.

THE HMAS *KUTTABUL* TRAGEDY

A monument to more recent history is on the eastern edge of the island, which looks out onto the harbour and the Heads. This was the scene of the one and only occasion when Sydney Harbour was invaded. It was here, on May 31 1942, that two Japanese midget subs entered the harbour (a third became entangled in anti-submarine netting near Camp Cove). One sub fired a torpedo at an American ship, the USS *Chicago*, moored in the harbour. The torpedo missed but it accidentally hit the HMAS *Kuttabul*, an old Sydney ferry being used as a floating barracks. Twenty-one sailors were killed (many more on board miraculously escaped injury) and their names are listed on this monument placed on the exact spot where they died.

The battered remains of two of the subs were found. Various parts have been stuck together and displayed at the War Memorial in Canberra, but the conning tower of the second sub, sliced like a fillet of fish, is on display at Garden Island, next to the small museum.

It is a revelation. Once you see the sardine can space in which two Japanese submariners (who must have been chosen for their size as well as their bravery) were supposed to exist for up to forty hours, you can appreciate that, like their brothers the kamikaze pilots, midget submariners did not expect to emerge alive. None of the Sydney attackers survived their mission.

Recently, a group of former World War II Japanese sailors and submariners were invited back to Garden Island to perform a sacred funeral ceremony at the remains of the midget sub. Memorabilia from this period is also included in the small museum located next to the conning tower. It is hoped that the museum will move to a much larger complex when plans to open up the historic section of Garden Island are finalised.

AUSTRALIA'S FIRST GRAFFITI?

The most historic location at Garden Island is on the hill which also features the first tennis courts built in Australia. Here is an outcrop of rocks overlooking the harbour, a favourite spot for sailors to sit and relax and, probably, wonder what they were doing halfway across the world. Here, protected from the elements by a pyramid of perspex, are three sets of initials carved into the sandstone. They are dated 1778, which makes them the first recorded markings in Sydney by white settlers, and also the first local examples of graffiti.

The initials FM are believed to belong to Frederick Meredith, a sailor from HMS *Sirius* who was later to become Sydney's first police constable. Also on this original part of the island are several small artisans' cottages and (out of bounds to visitors) the gracious homes on the top of the hill currently occupied by senior naval officers and their families. The island is still in constant use and has the busy atmosphere of a suburb in its own right. Also off-limits are the war rooms, which are only to be used in a state of national emergency, but are ready, we are told, for immediate use. There is another section adjoining the Garden Island complex which, while not part of the tour, can be approached from a different angle. It's worth the extra effort.

CLARENS GARDENS

The historic Grecian gardens called Clarens, part of Sir James Martin's former estate, have somehow survived where his historic house hasn't.

Clarens Gardens overlooks the southern tip of the Graving Dock but is officially part of the Australian Navy's HMAS *Kuttabul* barracks. This accommodation and recreation complex was built in 1966 on the site of three former waterfront mansions, and named after the unfortunate ferry destroyed just a few hundred metres away. The *Kuttabul's* wheelhouse survived the explosion. It's on display just inside the front security gates on Wylde Street, opposite the intersection with Grantham Street.

HMAS *Kuttabul* is normally off-limits to civilians, so it's tricky but not impossible to get through these gates to see the historic gardens hidden inside. Heritage groups are allowed in for guided tours, but if you phone 02 9359 9111 and express polite interest, chances are something can be arranged. It worked for me.

When the Navy took over this site, the historic gardens first built in the 1850s were already in a state of disrepair. Today they are sandwiched between much more modern buildings, struggling to survive. The sea, which once lapped at the bottom, has been relocated a couple of hundred metres away. You have to use your imagination to visualise how this place must have looked when it was built, but it's easy to believe that this was once a private paradise.

Sir James Martin, a NSW Premier and Chief Justice, was also a member of the Byron Society and a keen classicist. We can assume he liked a good party. His favourite god was Dionysus, a bit of a swinger, and there were formerly many references to him throughout the garden, including statues. Built on several levels leading down to what used to be the water's edge,

Clarens was personally designed by Martin to recreate the gardens of ancient Greece. It cost him 20,000 pounds, serious money in those days.

Originally there were thirty-eight sculptured urns here, but none have survived. The original focal point is also missing. An exact freestone replica of the Choragic Monument of Lysicartes dominated the middle garden before it was moved during World War II to the comparative safety of the lower lawn of the Botanic Gardens. There it still stands, possibly because the expense of moving it back (it had to be transported by barge) would be astronomical. It was thought the monument would be an easy target for enemy ships and planes.

While attempts are being made to keep what remains of the gardens intact, the feeling is that much of the original atmosphere has already been lost. A vent from a power substation intrudes into one section, a modern toilet block occupies another corner, and tall buildings block out the sunlight, making plant growth difficult. It has been estimated that it would cost well over a million dollars to fully restore (not including moving the sea back to its original position).

What remains is the basic structure, notably a series of magnificent sand-stone steps scaling the rock wall. The Temple of the Winds, a small shelter designed for Victorian ladies to sit in the shade and read verse, has also been saved. The solitary cabbage tree palm rising from the middle level is thought to be one of the few original plantings, possibly older than the garden itself.

Also of interest to stickybeaks is the privately-owned block of Spanish mission-style apartments immediately to the right of the gardens. The rich and the famous live here. The top flat, overlooking the gardens, the dry dock and the harbour, is the residence of Dame Joan Sutherland when she visits Sydney. It's rumoured Tom Kenneally also owns an apartment here.

Down on terra firma, this space is normally reserved for the fortunate navy personnel who can relax here during lunchbreaks. In some ways this is part of a long tradition, as Sir James Martin also liked to entertain visiting commodores in his spectacular Greek gardens. Perhaps he would have even approved of the latest naval additions. There is now an electric barbeque on the lower level, and at the very bottom, where once stood Martin's private bathing pavilion, there is now a volleyball court.

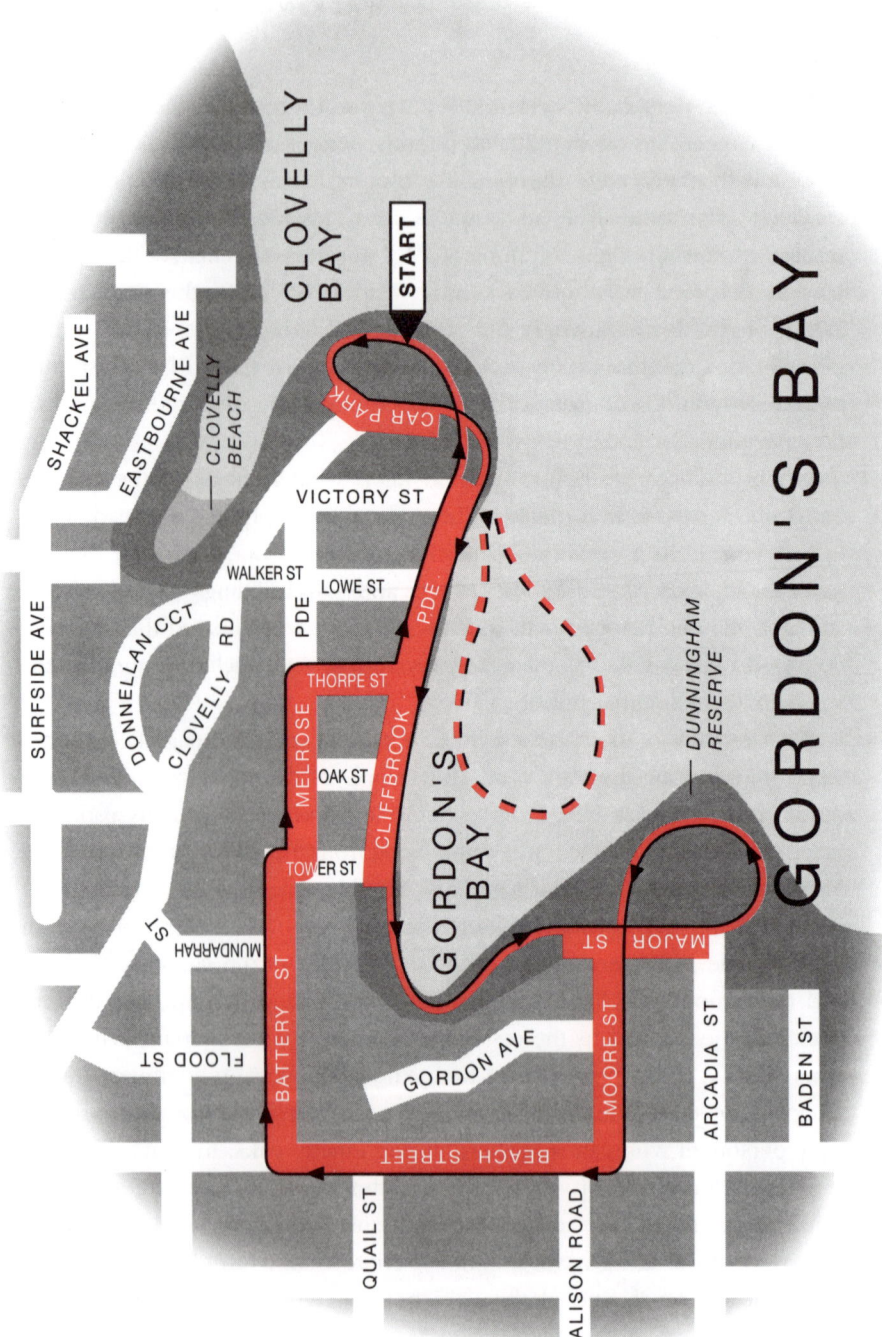

CLOVELLY BAY

GORDON'S BAY

GORDON'S BAY

START

CAR PARK

SHACKEL AVE

EASTBOURNE AVE

CLOVELLY BEACH

SURFSIDE AVE

DONNELLAN CCT

CLOVELLY RD

VICTORY ST

WALKER ST

LOWE ST

PDE

PDE

THORPE ST

MELROSE

OAK ST

CLIFFBROOK

TOWER ST

MUNDARRAH ST

FLOOD ST

BATTERY ST

GORDON AVE

MOORE ST

BEACH STREET

MAJOR ST

DUNNINGHAM RESERVE

ARCADIA ST

BADEN ST

QUAIL ST

ALISON ROAD

WALKING
GORDON'S
BAY

SUMMARY: *This circular walk around the edge of a tiny cove is surrounded by a fascinating history, including circus animals, a hermit, smuggling and the Prickly Pear Poison scandal of the 1920s. For the adventurous, this 'walk' can also be done underwater, following a length of sunken chain. Here's a chance to meet Sydney's friendliest fish, the beautiful blue gropers, noted for their ability to change sex if necessary. The Gordon's Bay walk contains several steep sections of steps and is unsuitable for wheelchairs. There are toilet facilities and dressing rooms at Clovelly Pool.*

START AND FINISH: *Car park at end of Clovelly Road, terminus for Sydney Buses 339 and 340.*

LENGTH: *One and a half kilometres, including one medium climb and descent.*

TIME: *One hour.*

REFRESHMENTS: *The excellent 'Cloey'—Clovelly Hotel, fifty metres from the car park; the seafood bistro is recommended. The cafes of Coogee are also within easy walking distance.*

There are two ways to see Gordon's Bay, the small, secluded section of coast between Clovelly and Coogee. The conventional method is via the short, undulating section of coastal path and boardwalk (called Cliffbrook Parade in street directories)—maybe 300 metres in length. This is the popular choice for joggers and dog owners, and on sunny Sunday mornings there can be human gridlocks on the narrower sections.

The less crowded approach is to do it underwater.

THE UNDERWATER TOUR

Gordon's Bay has long been a popular spot for scuba divers and snorkellers, but a recent innovation is the instalment of what is called an 'underwater path'—620 metres of chain kept in place with drums filled with concrete. The idea is that scuba divers (and on clear days, snorkellers) can follow the chain and be able to enjoy the best views of this unique marine environment.

The theory is that these man-made additions will eventually become covered with weed and blend in with their surroundings. The underwater trail starts at the end of the concrete pathway leading to the water at south-western corner of the Clovelly Beach car park. Further details from the Gordon's Bay Scuba Diving Club, PO Box 2192, Clovelly, NSW 2031.

BLUEY THE GROPER

One of the main attractions for divers on this part of the coast is the chance of seeing an eastern blue groper (*Achoerodon gouldii*). These large, gentle, friendly fish have all the qualities of a pet. Some will come up to divers and nuzzle them with their Mick Jagger lips. The most famous groper, nicknamed Bluey, lives with a harem of female gropers in Clovelly Pool, the natural sea water rockpool just the other side of Clovelly Beach car park.

There have been a number of Blueys over the years. The most famous was a huge metre-long, battle-scarred veteran who, according to locals, had occupied the same territory for over two decades. He disappeared a couple of years ago, and then, according to one of nature's miracles, one of his female followers suddenly changed sex (and colour) to take over the family.

The new Bluey is equally friendly to the hundreds of humans who dive down regularly to say hello. While Clovelly Pool, with its sharkproof net, is very popular with swimmers, Gordon's Bay, just a couple of hundred metres away, still has the quiet atmosphere of a Cornish smuggler's cove. The flotilla of multi-coloured tin boats pulled up on slips above the tiny sliver of sand are the sole reminder (along with the weathered shack belonging to Gordon's Bay Amateur Fishing Club) that this was once the centre of a small but thriving fishing industry. The advent of modern net fishing put an end to the professional small boat fishermen of Gordon's.

The bay is also one of the last remaining areas of native coastal heathland in Sydney—or it was until alien weeds arrived and began to take over.

Recent attempts by volunteer groups of local environmentalists to rip out the foreign invaders (the dreaded lantana and mirror plant in particular) appear to have been successful. Many native plantings have recently been undertaken to restore the bay to its original beauty. Several generations of rubbish, including discarded fridges and other debris, have also been removed from the slopes.

Despite signs suggesting that this is not allowed, the secluded rocks lining the water are a popular spot for nude sunbaking, even during the depths of winter. Those easily shocked by the sight of forbidden flesh (which can only be seen in detail if you happen to bring along a powerful pair of binoculars) should be forewarned.

For others, the greatest danger is a collision with joggers wearing headphones, who seem to feel they have right of way over mere pedestrians. Not so, but try arguing the point.

WARNING: SEA MONSTERS

Among the legends surrounding this remarkable place are the tales of sea monsters, real and imaginary.

There is the story of the late Percy Cane, a local lobster fisherman, battling a huge deep sea octopus which had wrapped its tentacles around his tiny fishing boat. There are also stories of giant blue gropers, twice as big as Bluey, living around Wedding Cake Island, the rock outcrop just south of the bay.

Gordon's Bay also had its own recluse. Up until 1976 when it was finally demolished, Ella Schiller lived in one upstairs room of the Cliffbrook mansion while the rest of the building slowly crumbled around her. This house, designed in the flamboyant Italianate style, was the first home to be built at Gordon's Bay in 1859, when it sat in splendid isolation among eleven acres of virgin bushland. All that remains now are small sections of the steps leading down to the beach.

A second mansion, a less spectacular Edwardian structure also called Cliffbrook and built on the site of the first mansion's stables, still remains at No. 45 Beach Street (turn right at Moore Street just after the southern end of the coastal path, then right again at Beach Road—Cliffbrook is on the corner of Beach and Battery Streets). This building, now surrounded by unsympathetic modern structures, is currently owned by the University of New South Wales.

It houses, among other departments, the university's printing works, although one of its previous and more exotic uses is indicated on the white front gates, where the letters AAEC are fashioned in wrought iron. The initials stand for the Australian Atomic Energy Commission, which was once based here.

DUNNINGHAM RESERVE

Any walk around Gordon's Bay should include the cliffs along the headland just to the south, known as Dunningham Reserve. Here there are magnificent views of the Pacific Ocean and, in particular, the bombora (surf-speak for a partly submerged reef) just below. Those with vertigo are well advised to keep away from the edge of the cliffs, which drop dramatically into the ocean.

One section of cliff has an overhang resembling a diving board which, according to Sydney's colourful criminal history, has been known to be used on several occasions as a powerful form of persuasion, especially in retrieving gambling debts.

The trick is to dangle the victim upside down over the precipice until they suddenly agree to pay up monies owed—with interest. Works every time, so I'm told.

THE PRICKLY PEAR SCANDAL

A large number of criminal activities have gone on in this colourful part of Sydney, but none more sensational than the Prickly Pear Scandal of 1928.

This involved Hyman Goldstein, a Country Party (now National Party) politician who was head of the parliamentary committee investigating the collapse of a company claiming to have devised a poison that would eradicate prickly pear, the imported cactus that was then in plague proportions throughout parts of rural Australia. The poison, as it turned out, was a dud. The chairman of the company fled the country.

By this stage the scandal had reached the Supreme Court where Goldstein, who was later found to own shares in the company, was subpoenaed as a witness. He never got to tell his story. One morning he was found dead at the bottom of these cliffs. He was wearing his pyjamas.

The coroner gave a verdict of accidental death, although it isn't hard to think of other, more sinister scenarios. Ever since, this beautiful part of Sydney has retained the spice of corruption.

ELEPHANTS IN GORDON BAY!

Personally, whenever I go to Gordon's, I can't help thinking about the elephants. A friend who grew up in this area about forty years ago once told me that a prominent circus family owned a house overlooking the water and, when the circus wasn't on the road, they tethered the elephants on the front lawns overlooking the water. Memories sometimes play tricks, but the image is indelibly imprinted in his brain and, since telling me, in mine as well.

START

MALLETT ST

FOWLER ST

DERBY ST

CAMPERDOWN PARK

CHURCH ST

NORTHWOOD ST

ROBERTS ST

GIBBENS ST

HOPETOUN ST

FEDERATION RD

ST STEPHENS CEMETERY

AUSTRALIA ST

DENNISON ST

ST STEPHENS

ROSS ST

O'DEA RESERVE

SALISBURY RD

ST MARY ST

STAFFORD ST

CARDIGAN ST

BRIDGE RD

PARRAMATTA RD (GREAT WESTERN HWY)

CORUNNA RD

MACAULAY RD

NORTHUMBERLAND

PERCIVAL LA

STANMORE STATION

CORUNNA RD

WESTBOURNE ST

DOUGLAS ST

CRYSTAL ST

INNER WEST

Walking the

Inner West

Summary: *A rambling walk takes you through Sydney's inner western suburbs, and also back through time, to the halcyon days of Chesty Bond, horse transport, steam locomotives, bicycle racing, classic rock 'n' roll and a guided tour of the only surviving piano roll factory in the Southern Hemisphere. Guided tours of the factory can be arranged by phoning 02 9569 5128 and I have to admit, it was a much more fascinating trip than I imagined.*

Plus, pay a visit to the cemetery to see the grave that, some say, inspired one of Charles Dickens' most memorable characters.

Start: *Corner Parramatta Road and Mallett Street, Camperdown. Sydney Buses 413, 436 – 440, L38, 461, 480 – 483).*

Finish: *Crystal Street, near the intersection with Douglas Street. Short walk down Douglas Street to Stanmore Station on main west line. Short walk north up Crystal Street to Parramatta Road, and Sydney Buses as mentioned.*

Length: *Four kilometres.*

Time: *Three hours (allow half an hour for tour of Mastertouch factory).*

Refreshments: *Several local milk bars on way, small detour to the many restaurants on King Street, Newtown, while Australia's busiest McDonald's is on the corner of Parramatta Road and Bridge Road, Stanmore.*

Sydney's inner western suburbs have only recently been discovered by young professionals seeking small, cheap houses with ready access to the city. Traditionally, these were areas designated for factories and working class families—some might even have called them slums. Today it is more of a 'ghettocino', a world of chic cafes and overpriced antique shops selling, ironically, the same stuff the original inhabitants would have thrown out when they moved twenty or thirty years ago.

There is charm in these narrow streets, as young owners restore quaint terrace houses to something far exceeding their original glory. Fortunately, some of the area's rich history survives—if you know where to find it.

CHESTY BOND

If you start in the suburb of Camperdown, just a kilometre or two from the CBD, a walk down Mallett Street (just south of the intersection with Parramatta Road) will inspire full-on nostalgia among baby boomers.

A hundred metres down, on top of a factory chimney located a few metres down Hampshire Lane but clearly visible from Mallett Street, is a larger-than-life image of Chesty Bond.

This square-jawed, curly-haired character with his snowy white Bonds singlet was the quintessential symbol of rugged Australian manhood when he was first created in 1938 by J. Walter Thompson admen Ted Moloney and Sid Miller. Apparently his physical appearance was based on that of Max Whitehead, a champion footballer and wrestler from the Sydney suburb of, appropriately, Manly Beach.

Chesty Bond was originally featured in a comic strip in the Sydney *Sun* newspaper. He was the local equivalent to Popeye, capable of superhuman powers as soon as he slipped on his singlet (but very vulnerable on washdays). The Chesty Bond image faded from popularity in the swinging 1960s (he would have looked terrible with a Beatles haircut) but made a comeback of sorts in the 1980s when, perhaps to Chesty's horror, he and his trademark singlet were adopted by the gay and lesbian community. Then the ultimate sacrilege. The Bonds label was sold to the multinational Pacific Dunlop group. Chesty went corporate.

This chimney in Camperdown bears one of the few surviving images of the early Chesty Bond. It is now part of the University of Sydney complex but, to their credit, they have ensured that old Chesty remains untouched.

Another reminder of how Camperdown used to be is just around the corner (turn right at the intersection of Mallett and Fowler Streets and walk over to the small section of park at the intersection with Gibbens Street).

It is only comparatively recently that horses were replaced as the main source of transport in Sydney, and here, under the shade of some very impressive fig trees, lies a simple but moving memorial to the days when horses ruled the roads.

Called the Sullivan RSPCA Memorial, this structure used to be a horse trough, but it has since been filled in with concrete—horses are pretty scarce these days. Small plaques at either end tell the story behind the memorial: 'To honour James Sullivan, who lost his life on 23rd June, 1924, when trying to save his employer's horses from death by fire'.

Unless I am mistaken, what appears to be the former stables, now restored and used for human habitation, are just down the road in Gibbens Street. It was soon after this 1924 tragedy that horses were replaced by horsepower, although by 1932, when the Sydney Harbour Bridge was first opened, there were still enough around for 'horse and rider' to appear on the list of tolls. It cost threepence to cross over. Most people approaching the age of fifty can still fondly remember horse-drawn milk trucks as recently as the 1960s.

For those overcome with horse-driven nostalgia, a very pleasant cafe lies just the other side of this small green space which now divides Fowler Street into two sections. It's a good place to sit on a sunny day and stare out over the surprisingly green expanse of Camperdown Park.

CAMPERDOWN VELODROME

There are two more monuments to historic forms of transport within easy access. If you turn right at the western end of Fowler into Australia Street, then first left at Derby Street and left again at Ross Street, you will be walking past O'Dea Reserve, scene of the Camperdown Velodrome. You may wonder what a velodrome is doing in such a quiet backstreet in a residential suburb. Despite its 1930s ambience, the track is relatively modern, built in the 1970s after the track at Henson Park was redeveloped. Camperdown Velodrome staged some big meetings in the seventies, but it is now considered too short (and too dangerous) for serious racing. Currently, the local council is considering applications for developing the property.

If the gates are open, it's well worth a look to marvel at the angle of the banking in the corners, a combination of cycle racing and the wall-of-death thrill ride. You may wonder how anyone could ride around what appears to be a near vertical wall. Apparently there were many spectacular crashes.

OFF THE RAILS

Fifty metres away, at the intersection of Ross Street and Salisbury Road, is Sydney's only shop dedicated to the romance of train travel. Off the Rails, set up by Scott McGregor and Mark Meadows, is an impressive collection of railway memorabilia, including train and carriage fittings. If you've ever dreamt of converting your rumpus room into a first-class sleeper carriage, this is the place to go. Where else in Sydney can you buy a restored 1950s quadracycle (a motorcycle-engine-powered buggy used for track maintenance)? Now all you need is a few thousand metres of unused railway track.

CAMPERDOWN CEMETERY

At the corner of Ross and Salisbury, it's worthwhile to detour back to Australia Street, crossing Salisbury and heading south to the intersection, first left, with Federation Road. It borders onto Camperdown Memorial Rest Park which has one of Sydney's hidden treasures, the St Stephens Church and Camperdown Cemetery (main entrance is on Church Street).

This detour is only for those with, if you'll pardon the expression, a couple of hours to kill. The 1849 cemetery surrounding the gothic revival St Stephens church, designed in 1870 by colonial architect Edmund Blacket to replace an earlier smaller one he also designed, is so full of treasures as to need a chapter of its own. Better still, obtain a pamphlet from the church offices and spend the whole day here. Some of the graves predate this cemetery. Bodies were relocated here from former city cemeteries at George and Devonshire streets, where the Town Hall stands today.

King Street, the busy main road of Newtown, is at the other end of

Church Street where you can buy lunch and spend the afternoon checking out the graves. Far from being a macabre place, this graveyard is a popular spot for picnics, something which the church leaders openly encourage in order to deter vandals. At the risk of offending other buried celebrities, it's hard to beat the grave of Eliza Emily Donnithorne, thought to be the inspiration for Miss Havisham in Charles Dickens's *Great Expectations.*

Eliza was living in her father's mansion in King Street when she was jilted by her bridegroom who was never to be seen again. She demanded the wedding day breakfast table be left set and was often seen in the house wearing her wedding dress. The front door remained open, awaiting his return. It was said she didn't leave the house until she died, in 1886, of a broken heart. These details are thought to have been relayed to Dickens by his son, who was visiting Australia at this time.

Other graves of note include those of the victims of the *Dunbar* and *Catherine Adamson* shipwrecks, plus one which features the blade of a ship's propellor.

Meanwhile, for those on the move, there are further treasures way out west, and the directions are, back to Salisbury Road and walk westward for 300 metres to Bridge Road, then turn right until you reach Parramatta Road.

AUSTRALIA'S BUSIEST McDONALD'S

The McDonald's on the corner of Parramatta and Bridge looks just like any other but it has a unique claim to fame. This is the busiest in Australia, selling more Big Macs than any other. Being open twenty-four hours a day helps.

Just before you reach McDonald's, chances are you would have been tempted by a food smell much more seductive than cheeseburgers. The World's Finest Chocolate factory is on the corner of Corunna and Bridge roads and on a day with favourable winds, its aromas have been known to drive chocaholics crazy as far away as Glebe. Tragically, the factory is now closed (but not for lack of my support). Can't say whether they really were the World's Finest Chocolates—as their name proudly boasted—but they were certainly Sydney's cheapest if you bought them direct from the factory.

A feature of many areas of the inner west was the names of streets spelt out in brick letters on corners, a reminder of the days when pedestrians were considered more important than motorists. The corner of Corunna Road and Bridge Road has a fine example of this long-lost artform.

Parramatta Road is normally an unpleasant place full of bumper-to-bumper traffic, but the section between Bridge Road and Northumberland Avenue is unique, featuring shops that are well worth braving the noise and carbon monoxide fumes.

ANTIQUES GALORE

At No. 76 (on the south side of Parramatta Road) is Photoantiques, which specialises in vintage cameras, radios and gramophones. Immediately across the road (warning: use the traffic lights if you want to survive the crossing) is Jackson's Rare Guitars. Both of these shops are virtual museums and, while everything is for sale, browsers are also welcome.

Steve Jackson's guitar shop is world famous and justifiably so. Classic guitars like the Les Paul Custom, the Fender Jaguar and the Gene Autrey acoustic grace the walls. Old guitars, especially those with history (which usually means someone famous once played it), are now worth a fortune. There are stories of guitars bought for a hundred dollars twenty years ago now fetching half a million at auction.

Many rock celebrities have made a point of checking out Steve's shop when they are in town, while one actually works here, namely Mark Evans, the former AC/DC bass player. The owner, Steve Jackson, is also a noted collector of vintage Holdens, especially the EK and FB models (circa 1960), hence the neat Holden panel van sign hanging over the footpath.

The shop next door, the Vintage Record Cafe, also has its claim to fame. It's run by Bosco Bosanac, former member of the legendary surf band, The Atlantics. 'Bombora', their big instrumental hit of 1963, is widely regarded as a classic of the genre. Bosco sells vintage records and rock memorabilia in his cafe, which features what he calls his 'Atlantics shrine' in one corner.

There must be something about this stretch of road. Above Photoantiques there is another 1960s icon in residence. The Lewis Morley Photographers Showcase is a gallery run by one of the most famous photographers of that decade. Although he has exhibited a variety of work all over the world, Morley is (to his partial frustration) best-known for one shot, that of a nude Christine Keeler—the girl involved in the Profumo scandal—straddling a chair. The pose is undoubtedly one of the most recognisable images of this century, and one of the most widely imitated, most recently by the Spice Girls in their stage show. Yet Morley remembers it like this: 'I rapidly shot off one roll of film with Christine posing nude in the chair. Eleven frames were exposed—the first one misfired—and it was all over in five minutes. The rest is history.'

Lewis Morley moved to Sydney from London in 1971 and, now semi-retired, likes to help young local photographers by displaying their work in his gallery. If you insist, you can also buy a signed Christine Keeler print.

There are other shops of interest in this stretch of Parramatta Road, although the wonderfully named House of Pain (it's a tattoo parlour) is only recommended to the adventurous. Walking westward, turn left at Northumberland Avenue, then right again at Corunna Road, for a hundred metres away is one of the most unusual houses in Sydney.

THE CHIMNEY HOUSE

It's hard to miss. No. 125 Corunna Road (on the corner of Percival Lane)—it features a giant chimney in its front garden. The chimney, dated 1900, belongs to the Metropolitan Board of Water Supply and Sewerage. Looking as if it escaped from a nearby factory, this is one of a series of outlets to allow gas to escape from the underground sewer. As befits something built in Queen Victoria's reign, this is no ordinary pipe, beautifully decorated with ornamental brickwork at the top. It is, however, very, very big and almost dwarfs the small cottage which looks as if it has been constructed around the pipe.

The chimney house has already been celebrated in print, being featured on p. 32 of John Belot's 1978 book, *Our Glorious Home*, a collection of photos of Australia's most extraordinary houses and gardens. Frustratingly, Belot neglected to tell readers where any of his discoveries were located, so for anyone who, like me, has always wondered where the small house with the big chimney is, look no further.

THE MASTERTOUCH FACTORY

There is one other secret location worth seeking out in the inner west and (providing you book in advance) it's well worth leaving till last. If you walk to the western end of Corruna Road and turn left at Crystal Street (you are now in the suburb of Petersham), you will notice a small factory at No. 96 called Mastertouch. It's directly opposite the intersection of Crystal and Douglas Streets, yet few people sitting in their cars waiting for the lights to change would realise that they are staring at the only surviving manufacturer of piano rolls in the Southern Hemisphere.

Piano rolls? Before CDs, before vinyl records, before 78s, people listened to piano rolls, and sang along. Remember pumping the pedals of a player piano in a pub and watching the keys move as if by magic? There is still a small but devoted cult of player piano enthusiasts and Mastertouch is keeping their pianos pumping.

Mastertouch has been manufacturing piano rolls since 1919 and inside is a range of more than 9,000 rolls for sale. Most of these are classics, like 'Kiss Me Goodnight Sergeant Major' and 'Zing Went the Strings of My Heart', but there are some surprisingly modern additions. Songs made popular by the Beatles, Billy Joel and Elton John have been re-recorded by Mastertouch. There's a wide variety of Elvis songs. 'She Loves You, Yeah, Yeah' is available on piano roll but, sorry, no silverchair as yet.

Most of the original recording equipment, now impossible to replace, is still used to cut the intricate series of perforations in the plain brown wrapping paper which magically creates music. These days computers are used to save time but the bulk of the technology is still unashamedly Edwardian.

The original Beale piano is still used to create the master roll. It sits proudly in Mastertouch's tiny recording studio. In the early part of this century, many musical legends sat at this piano. Australian virtuoso Percy Grainger was a notable advocate of the piano roll (early musicians saw this as a much more faithful means of recording than whatever else was available at the time) and many of the rolls he personally mastered are still available. Lesser-known pianists were used to record most of the music featured on rolls. The most legendary of these was Lettie Keyes (this was her real name, so I'm assured) who spent most of her musical career in the Mastertouch studio. She may well be the most recorded pianist in Australia, yet she remains virtually unknown.

For those interested in enjoying a roll or two in the privacy of their own home, pre-loved player pianos are still to be found, quite cheaply, in junk shops. These can be restored to perfect working order by one of several specialist player piano restorers in Sydney. Further details from Mastertouch.

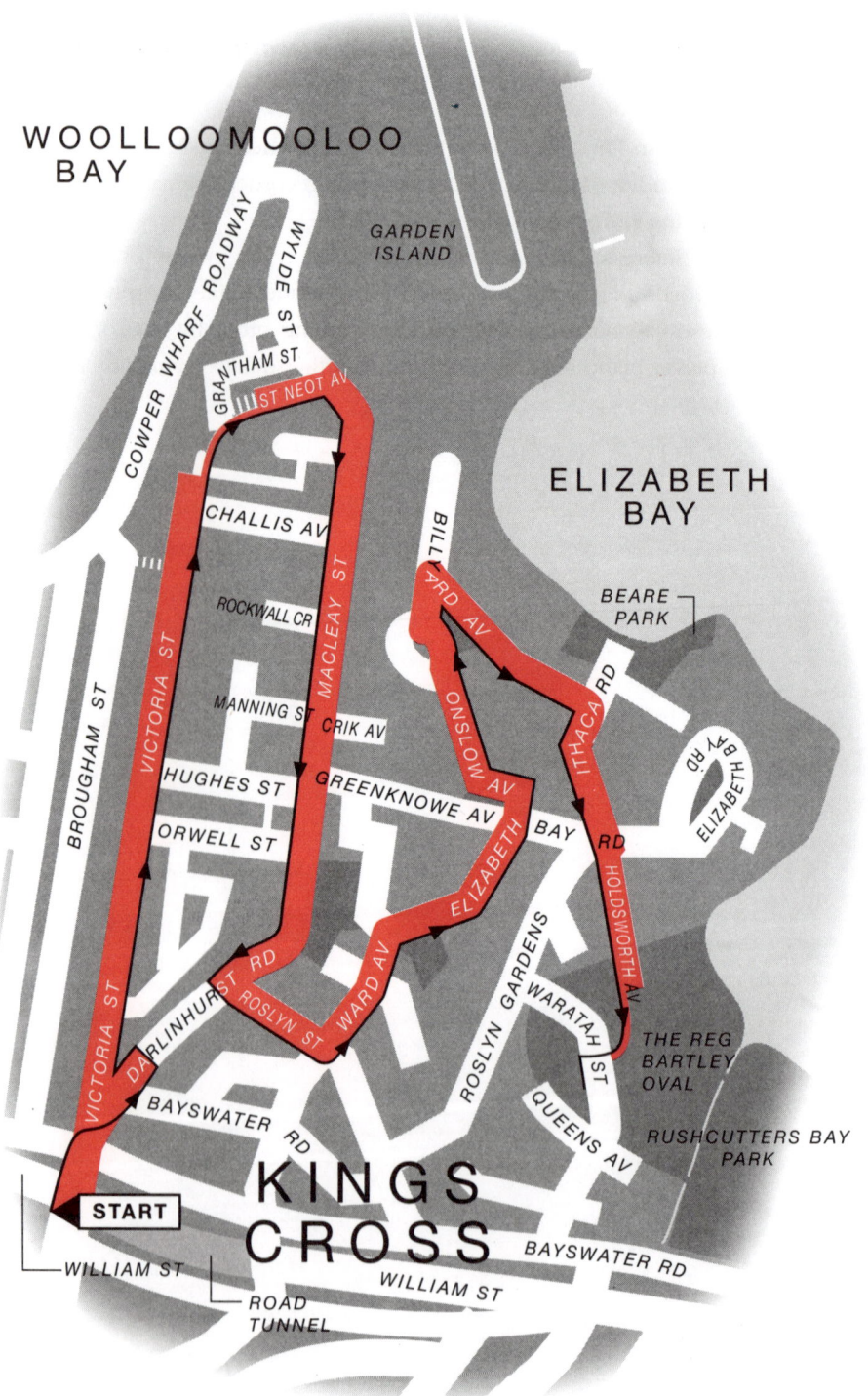

WOOLLOOMOOLOO BAY

GARDEN ISLAND

ELIZABETH BAY

BEARE PARK

COWPER WHARF ROADWAY

WYLDE ST

GRANTHAM ST

ST NEOT AV

CHALLIS AV

ROCKWALL CR

BILLYARD AV

ITHACA RD

ELIZABETH BAY RD

BROUGHAM ST

VICTORIA ST

MACLEAY ST

MANNING ST

CRIK AV

ONSLOW AV

HUGHES ST

GREENKNOWE AV

ELIZABETH BAY RD

ORWELL ST

HOLDSWORTH AV

DARLINHURST RD

ROSLYN ST

WARD AV

ELIZABETH BAY

ROSLYN GARDENS

WARATAH ST

THE REG BARTLEY OVAL

VICTORIA ST

BAYSWATER RD

QUEENS AV

RUSHCUTTERS BAY PARK

START

KINGS CROSS

WILLIAM ST

ROAD TUNNEL

WILLIAM ST

BAYSWATER RD

44

WALKING

KINGS
CROSS

SUMMARY: *A meandering walk takes you through what was once known as the Montmartre of Sydney, a suburb renowned for its bohemians, artists and eccentrics. Among other highlights are the former home of a witch, the site of Sydney's most enduring murder mystery, and the hotel balcony where the Beatles waved to their fans. Passing by several surviving art deco mansions and apartment blocks, end the walk at a charming kiosk to meet the Kings Cross cockatoo.*

START: *Above the Kings Cross tunnel on the corner William Street and Victoria Street (Kings Cross station on the Bondi Junction line; Sydney Buses 200, 327.)*

FINISH: *The tennis courts in Waratah Street (a short walk back to Kings Cross station, or buses 200, 327 at the end of Waratah Street and across footbridge to Craigend Street).*

LENGTH: *Three kilometres.*

TIME: *Two hours.*

REFRESHMENTS: *Countless cafes, shops and restaurants en route.*

I f you stand on the overpass above the Kings Cross tunnel, you are standing on the reason why they called this place Kings Cross. Well, not quite. The suburb was originally called Queens Cross, but when Queen Victoria died they decided to change the suburb's sex to suit the new monarch. There's a school of thought that it should be changed back to Queens Cross, and not only because Queen Elizabeth currently rules. It has more to do with the other kind of queen, but more about 'Les Girls' later.

The 'Cross' part of the name arose because two streets—William and Victoria—once intersected at this point. That was in a simpler age, before tunnels, high-rise apartment blocks and sex-change operations confused things. Now there are so many connecting streets at this point they should call it Kings Knot.

Another good reason to start here is so you can look down over the two lanes of traffic leading into and out of the tunnel. This is William Street, the direct line to the city that inspired the lines— 'you find this ugly, I find it lovely'—in Kenneth Slessor's poem. Slessor wrote 'William Street' in the 1930s, but his inspired descriptions of Kings Cross—'grease that blesses onions with a hiss'—are still relevant.

THE FERAL PALM

About ten years ago, a palm tree suddenly appeared and began to grow in the William Street median strip just below the overpass. It was a feral palm, growing wild in what was then a bare patch of weedy dirt. Despite the traffic and pollution and the lack of fertiliser, it just kept on growing. I followed its progress every time I drove through. The feral palm has since been joined by several others, courtesy of a beautification scheme by the local council. Thankfully, they left the original tree. It's easy to pick—it's ten years bigger than all the others.

Immediately behind you and across the road is the latest arrival on the Kings Cross cultural scene. In the courtyard in front of the new Elan tower is a sculpture by Ken Unsworth, opened in August 1998. The official title is 'Stones against the Sky', but it took less than a week to acquire the nickname 'Meatballs on Sticks'. Time will tell whether it achieves the status of that other Kings Cross icon, the El Alamein Fountain a few metres north.

THE KOREAN BATHHOUSE

First stage of this walk is in the general direction of that famous fountain. At No. 111 Darlinghurst Road, just past the merger with Victoria Street, is the Hotel Capital. When a Korean hotel chain took over the building in 1994 they decided to install a traditional Korean (similar to Japanese) bathhouse. This was the first of its kind in Australia, complete with three communal baths (hot, cold and ginseng) plus sauna and massage facilities.

This complex is open to the public and, especially for those of us from different cultures, it is a fascinating experience. Those on a walk may want to save this pleasure for last, but while we're here, these are the rules in brief. First, choose male or female. Unlike some Japanese bathhouses, this one is segregated. Get naked. It's traditional, and polite, to have a shower before entering the pools. Maybe try the sauna, then plunge into the cool pool. Next the warm pool. Followed by the bubbling ginseng pool, which feels like relaxing in a boiling cup of tea. Finally, if you have time, try a massage. For women (so I'm reliably informed), this luxury includes a sensual scrub down with yoghurt and honey.

When the bathhouse was opened in 1994, the manager was expecting a predominantly Asian clientele. He has been pleasantly surprised at the willingness of Australians to participate. This is hardly surprising as Kings Cross has always been a cosmopolitan culture. Australia's first Japanese restaurant opened here in the 1950s. The Korean bathhouse costs $20 to enter, a little extra for the massage. For full details, phone the Hotel Capital.

The next stage of our walk continues down Victoria Street. Technically, we are already in another suburb, Potts Point, although many say it feels more like Paris. It's the elm trees.

JUANITA NIELSEN'S HOUSE

A short way down on the right is a small terrace house at No. 202. This is the former home of Juanita Nielsen. She featured, and still does, in one of Sydney's great murder mysteries. On the morning of July 4 1975, Juanita left this house wearing a red leather coat and a brown beret. As usual, she was hard not to notice. She had an appointment at the Carousel Cabaret in Roslyn Street to discuss advertising in *Now*, the community newspaper she ran from home. Shortly after this meeting, she was seen getting into a yellow sedan driven by two men. She was never seen again.

The sinister background to this story concerns the very street you are now walking along. In the early 1970s, Victoria Street, lined with historic houses and graceful elm trees, was threatened by high-rise development plans that would have destroyed the prevailing atmosphere. The locals protested and green bans were put in place by unions. The developers hired thugs to put pressure on the residents. It was a virtual war.

Juanita Nielsen was firmly on the side of the residents. Quite rightly so, as her residence at No. 202 would have been one of the first to go.

Two men were eventually found guilty of conspiracy to abduct Juanita Nielsen but that didn't solve the mystery of what happened to her. The popular theory is that she was taken to a Kings Cross motel, murdered by a notorious ex-cop, and fed into a garbage disposal unit.

Juanita Nielsen, the heiress to a department store fortune, has since been commemorated by having a recreation centre for underprivileged kids named after her. But her true legacy is this street. Without her, it wouldn't be worth walking down.

For example, on the left side at No. 171, the Piccadilly Hotel is a beautiful pub. It serves as the meeting place of the Art Deco Society of NSW, a group which organises tours in July and August of the art deco buildings around Kings Cross. A surprising number have been saved from developers who will stop at nothing, including murder, to tear down old buildings. If you like Art Deco, phone 02 9319 1122 for details of these tours.

THE WITCH OF KINGS CROSS

For some reason, Kings Cross has a strong female presence. If this is Juanita's street, then the one parallel to it on your left belongs to Rosaleen Norton. Rosie was the official Witch of Kings Cross. Her former home, and coven, at No. 179 Brougham Street has since been replaced by town houses but a brief excerpt from her biography, *Pan's Daughter*, captures the magic (black, of course) of her pad.

'Rosie's and Gavin's room was full of clutter—animal skulls, bones, shells and stones lay strewn around amid discarded cigarette cartons and forgotten coffee cups. Broken battens in the ceiling had caused the plaster to flake and crumble, and cobwebs now adorned the dimmer recesses of the room. But even in these circumstances Rosie was able to ham it up a little, reinforcing her growing image as an eccentric. A sign in the corridor outside her flat read 'The Female Vagrant' and a placard on the door proclaimed: "Welcome to the house of ghosts, goblins, werewolves, vampires, witches, wizards and poltergeists".'

EMBARKATION POINT

Back to reality and towards the end of Victoria Street, just past the famous steps down to the Finger Wharf, is Sydney's newest green space. This one is unique. It is situated, literally, on the roof of a multistorey car park.

This may not be the most ideal of conditions in the world for plant growth but it does have some stirring views over the Sydney CBD and any visiting naval vessels.

This area was called 'The Park With No Name' until an official naming ceremony was held in July 1998. They chose Embarkation Park because this was the spot (before the car park) from which soldiers and sailors left to serve in the two world wars.

Not everyone thought this was such a great name. A group of locals had lobbied for it to be called Phil Bartlett Park, after a local newsagent who was senselessly shot by an intruder in 1983. It was a nice thought, but as the park is on land owned by the Navy, Embarkation Park it is.

The car park was built in 1984 for personnel at Garden Island and has long been considered one of the suburb's eyesores. At least the roof is now aesthetically pleasing.

The continuation of Victoria Street leads to a paved brick pathway that turns right and ends at steps leading up to St Neot Avenue. This corner pocket of the Cross shows what the entire suburb was once like. More like the back streets of Chelsea than Sydney in the 1940s and 1950s, the suburb was known as the bohemian capital of Australia on account of those who lived in these once cheap flats. Artists and writers still live here, but only if they have well-paid day jobs as lawyers and art directors to pay the rent.

THE YELLOW HOUSE

A right turn at St Neot follows the curved front of an apartment block much-loved by architects. We are now in Macleay Street, and at No. 59 is the building known as 'the Yellow House' in the late 1960s and early 1970s. This was Sydney's equivalent to Andy Warhol's Factory, a place for artists to get together and experiment. Martin Sharp, Tiny Tim, Brett Whiteley, George Gittoes, Nell Campbell, Robert Hughes and Roger 'Ellis D. Fogg' Foley were among those who lived, worked and performed here. While most of the above became rich and famous, the house (no longer painted yellow) is now used for low-rent accommodation.

During my research, I was told that some of the murals painted by Brett Whiteley during his Yellow House period are still on the walls. I couldn't get inside to verify this claim, but if it is true, the market value of the building has just risen by a million or two.

THE BEATLES STAYED HERE

Across the road at No. 40 is another reminder of the swinging 1960s. Now the Astor Macleay Executive Apartments, it was formerly the Sheraton Wentworth Hotel where the Beatles stayed during their 1964 Australian tour.

The Fab Four took over the entire top floor while their fans stood (or collapsed) on the footpath below. There has been nothing like this since. Girls had to be restrained from climbing up the front of the building.

The balcony where the Beatles stood and waved to their fans is still pretty much as it was. You can still imagine John Lennon up there, giving his trademark Nazi salute. This section of Macleay Street has a wild reputation. Directly opposite is a new hotel that replaced one called the Chevron. It was in that hotel that Marianne Faithfull attempted suicide in 1969. She was staying on the 13th floor with Mick Jagger.

Further down Macleay Street, two more wild slices of the 1960s. Turn right into Hughes Street and you'll see the Wayside Chapel, launched in 1963 by the late Reverend Ted Noffs to cater to the 'Beatles, beatniks and bohemians' of the Cross. Forty years on and this is still somewhere for the lost and the lonely to get help. Noffs claimed that his chapel was the most popular place for weddings in the world. Out front is the Peace Garden.

Orwell Lane, next to the chapel, leads you to one of the Art Deco Society's great delights. The wonderful Metro Theatre on the corner of Orwell Street and Orwell Lane is most famous as the stage for the Australian production of *Hair*. Starting in 1969, the crowds—and the censors—lined up here waiting to see the world's first hippie-love-rock-musical. This production launched the career of Marcia Hines, among others.

HOME OF THE STEAK SINATRA

Music of another sort emanated from the Bourbon and Beefsteak, at No. 24 Darlinghurst Road, just after grand old Macleay Street passes the fountain, turns the corner and changes its name. The B&B marks the start of the sleazy side of the Cross. According to local legend, this celebrated New York-style restaurant and bar (it never closes) was built to make visiting crime lords feel at home. True or not, the decor, which has to be seen to be believed, can best be described as Mafia Moderne.

While packed with drunk-as-skunks sales reps most weekends, this is still the only place in town where you can order a Steak Sinatra, the dish named in honour of ol' blue eyes when he visited Sydney in 1974. Best with a Bloody Mary or two.

At time of writing, the Bourbon and Beefsteak floor show was being provided by Carlotta and Her Beautiful Boys. Carlotta, the true Queen of the Cross, is Australia's best-known drag artiste.

Her spiritual throne is just a few doors down on the corner of Darlinghurst Road and Roslyn Street. This was the home of 'Les Girls' (with Carlotta as the star of the show) for over thirty years. The idea of a cabaret featuring boys dressed as girls originally started as a short-term gimmick. The gimmick lasted thirty years before the public tired of the novelty.

There were wild scenes in here. Carlotta tells me there is still a bullet hole in the ceiling from when a local crim got over excited.

THE PICCOLO BAR

A walk along Roslyn Street takes you past the Piccolo Bar, established in 1950 and one of the first coffee shops in Australia. Still worth a visit and one of the few to keep its authentic bohemian atmosphere.

After the Piccolo, turn left at Ward Avenue which becomes Elizabeth Bay Road, and head towards Art Deco heaven. But first, at the corner where Greenknowe Avenue, Elizabeth Bay Road and Onslow Avenue collide, there is Sydney's smallest park. Despite its postage-stamp size, this park contains a constantly flowing waterfall. A sign warns that camping is not allowed.

ARTHUR McELHONE RESERVE

The walk down Onslow Avenue passes Elizabeth Bay House on one side and the Arthur McElhone Reserve on the other. This beautiful but largely unknown park is designed in a Japanese style, complete with ornamental fish ponds. Despite being in the heart of one of the most densely populated parts of Sydney, it remains an oasis of calm with a clear view over the harbour. A picnic in Kings Cross? This is the place.

The road beneath the park is Billyard Avenue, which winds downhill to meet Ithaca Road. On this corner is what the Art Deco Society considers our finest example of Spanish mission architecture—and there's no argument from me. The mansion known as 'Boomerang' was designed in 1926 by Neville Hampson for Frank Albert, a gentleman who made his considerable fortune from selling sheet music and mouth organs.

Albert's most popular items were a series of Boomerang Songbooks which inspired the name of the house and also the boomerang motif throughout. This is a private residence but the Art Deco Society runs occasional guided tours of the house, as they do with two more master-pieces of the genre, which can be seen by walking up Ithaca Road and turning left at the continuation of Elizabeth Bay Road. The ones to look out for are at Nos. 63 and 68.

THE KINGS CROSS COCKATOOS

Directly opposite the end of Ithaca Road is a small lane called Holdsworth Avenue, which leads to a series of steps down to Rushcutters Bay Park. An avenue of trees behind the old grandstand overlooking Reg Bartley Oval (the grandstand is thought to be the oldest in Sydney) takes you to one of the true gems of the Kings Cross area. Just across Waratah Street from the grandstand are the small octagonal kiosk and outdoor tea rooms belonging to the Rushcutters Bay Tennis Courts. Looking like something from the 1920s, this kiosk is the ideal place to end a walk. This is where you can meet the Kings Cross Cockatoo.

Rory Miles, the resident coach at Rushcutters, has a number of interests apart from tennis. He collects micro cars, he grows bonsai trees and he keeps cockatoos, especially ones that can talk.

Sasha is his latest bird, a three-year-old Major Mitchell who is becoming a local identity. He has taken over the perch from Peter, his much-loved predecessor at the kiosk. Peter, as ridiculous as it may sound, was stolen.

By the way, Sasha is a he, following in that fine Kings Cross tradition of boys with girls' names. When he fluffs up his coral pink feathers, he looks as if he just stepped off a Mardi Gras float.

These tennis courts (available for hire to the public) are also the home of another female legend. Lesley Bowery is a regular player here. When she was known as Lesley Turner she won a couple of French Opens. Such is her skill on slow clay courts that she managed to beat Margaret Court, by far the best female player of that period. Rory Miles takes great delight in setting up matches between Mrs Bowery and men half her age. Rory says it's a good way to teach young upstarts a bit of humility.

You may notice a photo of radio star John Laws on the wall of the kiosk. This is Rory Miles' other claim to fame. He's Lawsie's tennis coach as well.

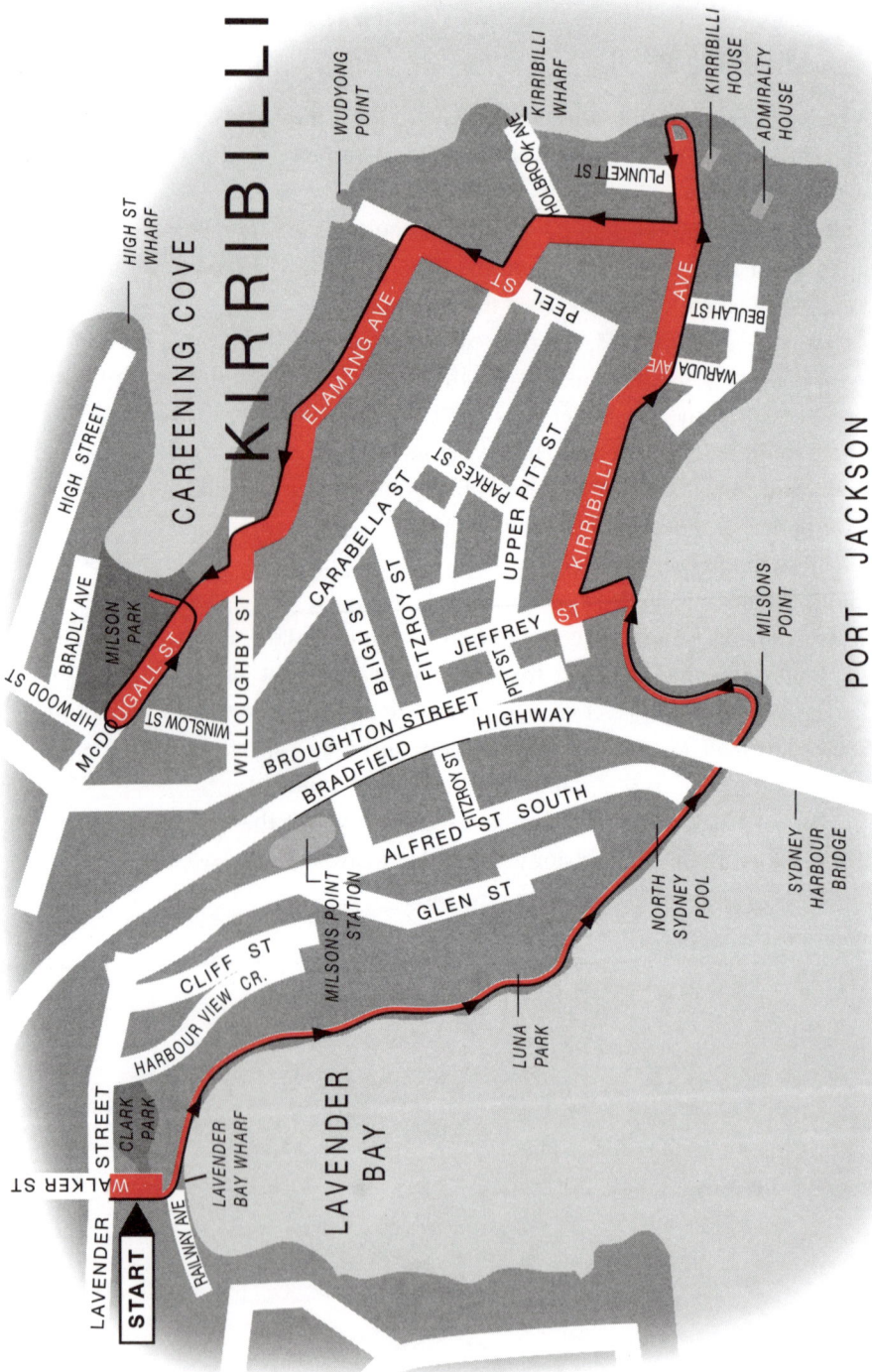

Walking
Lavender Bay
and
Kirribilli

Summary: *This is a walk following the northern foreshore underneath Sydney Harbour Bridge, starting at the former home of Australia's best-known modern artist, passing the Luna Park amusement centre and the Prime Minister's residence. If you are lucky enough to be walking in November, here's a chance to walk under Sydney's most spectacular tunnel of jacaranda trees before celebrating with a quiet drink on a balcony overlooking the harbour.*

Start: *Walker Street, Lavender Bay (North Sydney Station on North Shore Line; Sydney Buses 228–230; Hegarty's Lavender Bay Ferry from Wharf 6, Circular Quay).*

Finish: *Milson Park (short walk to High Street Wharf or Kirribilli Wharf, on Sydney Ferry's Neutral Bay run; short walk up Willoughby Street to Milsons Point station).*

Length: *Three kilometres.*

Time: *Two hours.*

Refreshments: *At North Sydney, near the train station; at Milson's Point, near the station; and at the Sydney Flying Squadron, a licensed club serving food and alcohol.*

The late Brett Whiteley, Sydney's best-known modern artist, has a couple of permanent memorials in Sydney. The big matchsticks (one burnt, one not—his personal yin and yang symbol) stand behind the Art Gallery of NSW, while his former studio in Raper Street, Surry Hills is now a public gallery devoted to his life and work.

There is another lesser-known Whiteley landmark. His spectacular home at Lavender Bay (not open to the public) is in Clark Park at the bottom of the steps leading towards Lavender Bay Jetty. The steps begin at the intersection of Walker Street (which leads to North Sydney Railway Station) and Lavender Street.

Whiteley's house was the white house, the one closest to the water's edge, easily distinguished by its round tower resembling a lighthouse. The view from the top, overlooking the waters of Lavender Bay and the bridge, featured in several of Whiteley's paintings. One of the artist's totem sculptures is visible over the front fence, as is a stair rail down the side made from driftwood.

A series of sculptures by other artists has been placed around the Whiteley house. My favourite is the tiny brass statue of Ginger Meggs, credited to Scott Edmunds, hiding in the gardens halfway down the steps. Meggs, an Australian cartoon character was created in the 1920s by Jim Bancks, a favourite icon of Whiteley and his contemporaries from the Yellow House group.

There are sculptures on the other side of the house that include a brass teapot engraved with the names of 1940s movie stars, and, nestling among the foliage, an African bust by Joel Ellenberg.

This is an unexpected open art gallery. At the bottom of the steps is Lavender Bay Wharf. Up until recently I thought the area was named after the many jacaranda trees planted around here that turning purple in November. A romantic notion, but not so.

This area originally went by the less romantic title of Hulk Bay, after the number of abandoned ships left here to rot. It was later changed to Lavender Bay after Captain George Lavender, who, to add to the colour theme, married the daughter of local identity Billy Blue. The nearby Blues Point was named after him.

THE LAVENDER BAY FERRIES

Anyone lucky enough to live near Lavender Bay can walk down the steps to the wharf to catch the small, vintage, blue and white Hegarty Brothers ferry to the city. The Lavender Bay ferry, also servicing Jeffrey Street and Beulah Street wharves, is one of the few remaining privately-owned ferry services in Sydney.

Hegarty's boats are old but full of charm, and this has to be one of the most pleasant ways to commute anywhere in the world. For tourists, this is the perfect opportunity to see the Sydney Harbour Bridge from a unique perspective—the boats travel underneath the bridge on the outwards journey from Circular Quay. When you arrive at Lavender Bay Wharf, you'll notice two fishing boats, the *Fair Star* and *Sicilia Star*, moored on each side of the jetty. These are working boats, still in use. There is a small, largely unnoticed fishing industry operating within sight of the Sydney CBD, catching fish at dawn.

At the bottom of the steps, there is an historic plaque on the rock wall close to the toilet blocks. This marks the site of Cavill's Baths, which existed here from 1881 to 1975. The Cavill family was headed by 'Professor' Fred Cavill, who swam the English Channel in 1877 and taught Princess Mary, the future Queen Mary, how to swim. Most of Cavill's many children were also famous for their swimming ability. His youngest son Dick, the first man to swim a hundred yards in less than a minute, is also acknowledged as being the first to use the Australian Crawl stroke (now better known as freestyle) in competition swimming.

Dick's brother Arthur is credited with inventing this stroke, perhaps by accident, when he accepted a challenge to swim with his feet tied together. Another Cavill sibling, Sydney, invented the butterfly stroke.

The sliver of land leading south from the wharf towards the bridge was private property until quite recently. It is still used by NSW Railways to store trains overnight but now there is a boardwalk allowing public access. It must be the world's most valuable train park. Walking along the tracks, one can wonder how much this chunk of prime real estate would be worth to a property developer. Which brings us to Luna Park, and the fantastic blue spires of Coney Island which, from this direction, dominate the horizon.

THE GHOSTS OF LUNA PARK

Sydney's most famous amusement park dates back to 1935 when the original rides were transported here, by ship, from Adelaide. Old Uncle Luna has had a tragic couple of decades. The original slogan—'Just For Fun'—seems especially ironic these days. There were times when this unique amusement park, with its trademark Uncle Luna face, would attract a million and a half patrons a year. Ted Hopkins, the show man who built it, considered it the world's best, in the best location in the world. Those days are long gone.

After the Ghost Train tragedy in 1979 when six children and one adult died in a fire, Luna Park has been struggling for its existence. Closed and re-opened many times since, the place has been repainted and redesigned under the supervision of artist Martin Sharp (a friend of Whiteley's and also a member of the Yellow House group) who tried to preserve the spirit of the park.

A valiant effort, but the park was quickly forced to close after nearby residents complained about the noise levels of the new yellow Big Dipper. Sadly, at this time, this magic place remains shut. Fortunately, the Coney Island building is heritage-listed and remains in more or less its original condition. Inside are some large wooden slippery dips and, on the walls, priceless murals by comic artist Arthur Barton dating from the World War II period. Hopefully, one day this building will be open to the public again.

The famous Luna Park face is still there but like the mask he is, there's nothing going on behind. Uncle Luna is best seen from the water at night, or from the train crossing the bridge. The smile is a recent innovation, part of the many attempts to improve the park's image. The original face was positively demonic.

NORTH SYDNEY OLYMPIC POOL

Next to Luna Park is North Sydney Olympic Pool. This may be an Olympic-sized pool, with spectacular views of the harbour from the grandstand, but you won't see any Sydney 2000 events in here, partly because it's filled with seawater. A shame, as a little bit of seawater didn't stop Dawn Fraser setting several records in here. The outside walls of the pool (you'll see them best from the boardwalk) are nicely decorated with frogs, seagulls and swordfish. These have been painted in bright colours that match those of Luna Park. Another feature of this pool is the inflatable bubble that covers the water in winter months. It's a unique feeling to swim here on a cold rainy day—with steam from the heated pool creating a sauna effect. Try it, it's open to the public.

The road leading down the hill to the pool entrance is Alfred Street South, and a hundred metres up the hill is a unique monument. The ornamental archway across the road, spelling out Luna Park in neon on the far side, was constructed by the original amusement park management as a way of enticing people down the hill. It's the only privately owned roadway arch in Sydney.

HMAS *SYDNEY*

If you continue walking along the water's edge from North Sydney Pool, passing under the North Pylon of the bridge, you'll soon come to the bow of the original HMAS *Sydney*, a ship best known for sinking the German cruiser *Emden* in 1914. The bow has been sliced off like a piece of cheese and set into the harbour wall. This is one of a number of items of nautical memorabilia (some even more bizarre) placed around the harbour. Others of note are the mast of the HMAS *Sydney* set on the cliff at Bradley's Head, and the figurehead of Lord Nelson (which once graced an 1814 man-o'-war) at Rushcutters Bay. Strangest of all is a Doric column from the old GPO building set into shallow water at Bradley's Head. But this has a practical purpose, being used to measure one nautical mile from Fort Denison.

For those interested, these and other harbour mysteries are revealed in Cedric Emanuel's delightful *Sydney Harbour Sketchbook*, published by Rigby. Most libraries have a copy.

But back to what is now, once you have passed under the bridge, the suburb of Kirribilli. A walk uphill through Bradfield Park (quickly past the ventilator grilles that let out carbon monoxide fumes from the Sydney Harbour Tunnel) will take you to Kirribilli Avenue, which leads us to the most exclusive address in Sydney.

But before we leave the bridge, a quiet word of warning. A friend of mine was walking here one day when he found a bridge bolt the size of a toothpaste tube on the ground. I've never been able to walk under the bridge since without anxiously looking up.

NORTH SHORE'S FIRST BLOCK OF FLATS

Halfway down Kirribilli Avenue is Waruda Avenue which leads down to Waruda Street. At No. 1 Waruda Street (next to the park known as Dr Mary Booth Lookout) is a very solid-looking block of flats which must have some of the best views in Sydney. These are allegedly the first block of flats on the North Shore, built in 1908. They were originally owned by Mrs. James White, the owner of the Melbourne Cup winner, Carbine. At the time, living in a flat was seen as quite radical. There are still signs of their former grace but a recent modernisation is, in my opinion, a change for the worse.

KIRRIBILLI HOUSE

Towards the end of Kirribilli Avenue are the guarded gates to Kirribilli House and Admiralty House. Unless you've been invited there by the Prime Minister or Governor General you can't enter (although in 1998 a group of environmental protestors had little trouble getting in), but you can share a similar experience by following the road till it comes to a dead end at the small stepped park at Lady Gowrie Lookout. Here, only a wall separates you from the Prime Minister's private gardens. Bob Hawke liked to work out here on a banana lounge in his Speedos, but I can't imagine John Howard doing that. The park is usually empty except for the security guards who wander over to sit and have a quick cigarette on their breaks. Some are friendly and will fill you in on governmental gossip.

WALEY'S ARCH

From here a pleasant walk down tree-lined streets takes you right at Carabella Street and right again at Peel Street. At the end of Peel Street lies the Royal Sydney Yacht Squadron, a private club with even tighter security than Kirribilli House. Inside these grounds is another of those nautical curiosities featured in Cedric Emanuel's book, an archway constructed of the jawbones of a giant whale caught at Twofold Bay, near Eden on the south coast. These bones were given to the club early this century by a member called, appropriately enough, Waley.

If you can't get into the club to see Waley's Arch, you can see it from the Neutral Bay ferry, shortly after it leaves Kirribilli Wharf.

From near the end of Peel Street, Elamang Avenue takes you northwards, past the grounds of Loreto Convent school, to Milson Park, at the tip of Careening Cove. There is a fine old fig tree towards the end of Loreto Convent, but I can remember from first-hand experience, an even older, bigger tree next to it. I was living next door when it suddenly dropped down dead one dark and stormy night in the late 1980s, with a crash like thunder. It blocked the road but very politely missed my parked car by centimetres.

Just after Elamang Avenue ends and meets McDougall Street, you'll find the Ensemble Theatre, started up in the 1960s by American director Hayes Gordon. This is a rare 'intimate' theatre space, converted from an old warehouse, with a glass-walled restaurant over the water. The stage is tiny, surrounded on three sides by seats, but many fine Australian actors have launched their careers from this venue, Russell Crowe among them.

THE JACARANDA TUNNEL

Milson Park, fifty metres north of the Ensemble, has at least two claims to fame. One of them is blatantly obvious for a brief period towards the start of summer. The section of McDougall Street which borders the park is lined by two rows of jacaranda trees that explode with blossoms, usually in the first week of November (but with today's erratic climate, give or take a couple of weeks).

For the next few weeks, the jacaranda blossoms form a glorious purple tunnel which makes this a popular destination for coachloads of Asian tourists who can be seen risking injury by standing in the middle of the road aiming cameras. Just as spectacular, when the blossoms fall the road becomes a carpet of lavender.

At other times in summer, Milson Park is famous as the north-of-the-harbour headquarters for the uniquely Australian sport of eighteen-foot sailing (they've never gone metric and probably never will).

The sport has a rich tradition but from the beginning, these craft have been been raced by professionals. Most boats are fully sponsored. Eighteen-footers are considered the Formula Ones of sailing, understandably so, considering their phenomenal speed when racing on the harbour.

Nowadays the boat shells are made of carbon fibre and have a crew of three who, at speed, balance on trapeze-like wings built on either side of the boat. The boats are assembled and launched at Milson Park most summer Saturday afternoons, next to the Sydney Flying Squadron on McDougall Street. This licensed club is open to the public and features a waterfront balcony with spectacular water views, perfect for a quiet drink on a summer's evening. The club is virtually an eighteen-footer museum. The walls are lined with historic photos and a couple of old wooden yachts are kept in the shed at the bottom.

THE BOOKIE BOAT

It is also from here that you can catch the famous 'bookie boat', the historic red and yellow harbour ferry that takes spectators out on the harbour so they can see the yachts racing. There's a refreshment bar on board the boat and there is even a running commentary over the public address system. The boat is called the 'bookie boat' because it was once a Sydney tradition for a racecourse bookie to be on board, complete with white satchel and a betting board. It was all part of the fun to have a small wager on the yacht of your choice. Unfortunately, this novelty has been deemed technically illegal (these days only the NSW TAB is allowed to take your betting dollar), so this fine Sydney tradition is no more. Wagers are still made on the bookie boat, but privately, between friends.

Bookie or not, a trip on the harbour to see the flying eighteen-footers is one of Sydney's greatest summer delights. Flying, by the way, is not an exaggeration. Under spinnakers, the boats literally take off, bouncing into the air when they hit the aquatic equivalent of a speed bump.

For enquiries about the bookie boat (tickets are usually $10) and for race details, phone the Sydney Flying Club Squadron on 02 9955 8350. The boat is rarely crowded. Most weeks there is no need to book ahead.

Milson Park (or better still, the balcony of the Flying Squadron, with a celebratory schooner) marks the convenient end of this walk. Then it's a short stroll west up Willoughby Street to Milsons Point Railway Station (home, by the way, of an award-winning pie shop) or a short walk east (through the park) to the High Street Wharf for a scenic ferry ride back to Circular Quay.

WALKING
MINCHINBURY

SUMMARY: *A circular walk takes you around a typical new sub-division in Sydney's outer western suburbs. Based on the site of a former winery, a few symbols of its former use remain, including a row of one hundred ancient olive trees which once lined the original driveway. This is a chance to see the kind of new suburb in which the majority of Australians now live.*
START AND FINISH: *At the corner of Great Western Highway and Minchin Drive—look for 'the crashing plane'. Public transport is limited; nearest train station is Mount Druitt from which local buses to Minchinbury leave.*
LENGTH: *Two kilometres.*
TIME: *An hour and a half.*
REFRESHMENTS: *Supermarket and milk bar at Minchinbury Shopping Centre in Minchin Drive. McDonald's on corner of Great Western Highway and Colyton Road, about half a kilometre west of Minchin Drive.*

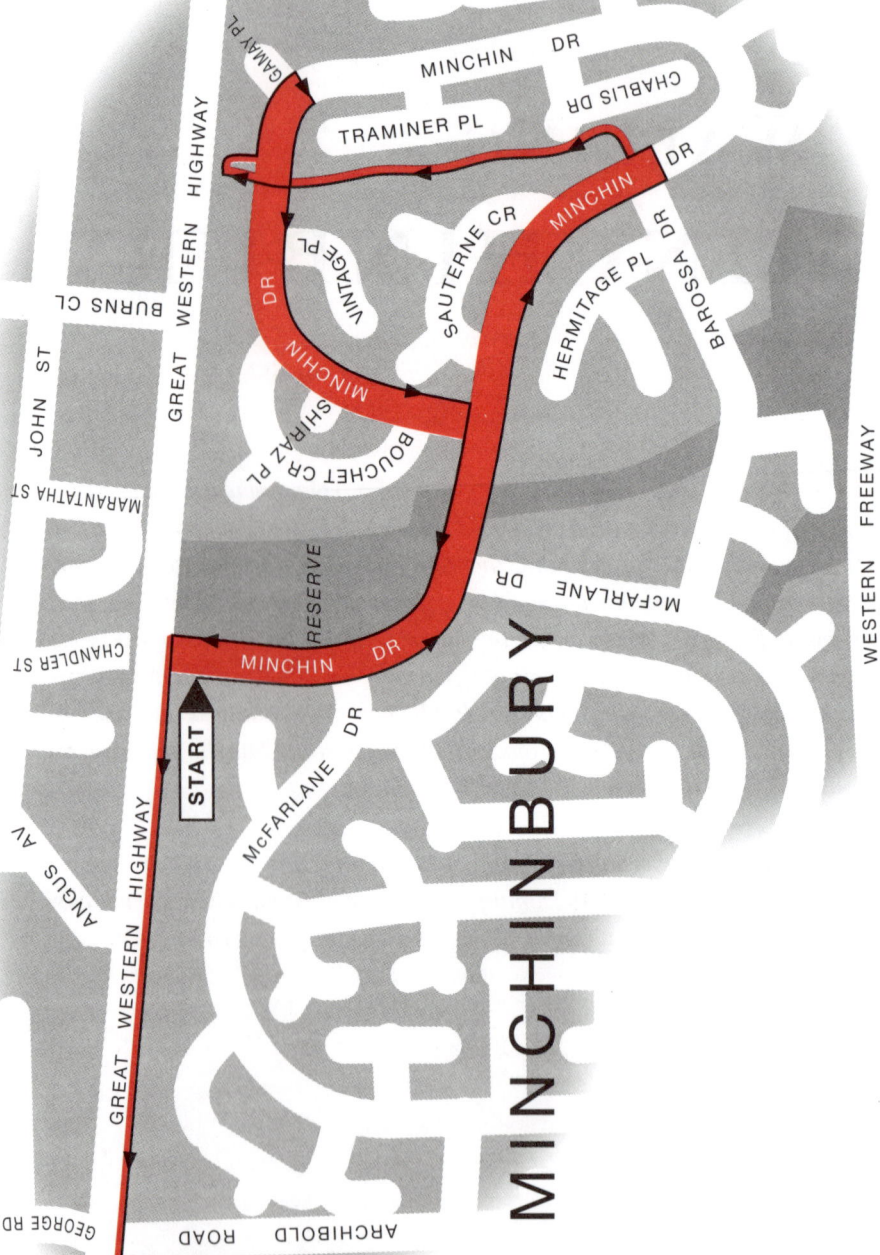

MINCHINBURY

START

The suburbs of Sydney have spread so far westward that Parramatta, more than twenty kilometres from the CBD, is now officially the geographical centre of Sydney. Thirty years ago, most people who lived out west would have done so in a house made of fibro. Some fine examples of fibro remain, mostly painted mint green, but these are relatively few in number. Today, people out west live in new brick houses.

Minchinbury, about thirty-five kilometres from the city off the Great Western Highway, is a typical new housing development. The suburb exists where there was none twenty years ago. Then, the place was full of grapes.

The site is a former Penfold's winery. Minchinbury was the name of the property (the original land grant was made to Captain William Minchin in 1819) and also a popular brand of champagne, in the days when France allowed foreigners to use that name for sparkling wine.

The winery, now derelict and fenced off, was closed in 1978. Apart from this brief historical connection, Minchinbury is the essence of the modern Australian suburb, the kind of place where 'Neighbours' might be filmed if the producers wanted to give their show a multicultural update. Migrants from Asia, the Middle East and the Pacific region make up the bulk of this community, although there is little indication of this in the architecture. I noticed a letterbox of a Chinese design, but that's about it. Today the signpost to Minchinbury estate, on the corner of the Great Western Highway and Minchin Drive, is obvious to anyone driving along the highway.

THE CRASHING PLANE

The 'crashing plane' mounted on a pole has been a feature of this location for over sixty years. There are several stories as to how the first crashing plane came to be here. The mystery has inspired spirited debate in local papers for years. One version is that a plane accidentally crashed here in the 1930s and was left as a monument.

The slightly more credible version is that a plane was erected on the site by Penfold's as an advertising gimmick. According to one report (Penfold's have no official records), the original aircraft, a single-engined monoplane, was sold to the winery in 1932 and erected on the site, nose downwards, with the slogan 'Don't Crash—Drink Penfold's Wines' painted on the wings.

This grounded aircraft apparently fooled the pilots of several passing planes who reported the crash-landing to airport authorities. The original plane was destroyed in the 1940s by a severe wind storm. A replica was destroyed soon afterwards by fire or vandals (probably both) before being replaced by the current model. This plane, a replica of a streamlined jet, was restored by members of the Mount Druitt Historical Society and placed back on its plinth in 1988.

Just as employees of the old vineyard would tell visitors to 'drive over the hill and turn left at the plane crash', so too can current residents.

This then is the start point of any walk around Minchinbury. Many of the streets have been named with a wine theme (Traminer Place, Alicante Street, Shiraz Place) but the two most obvious connections with the winery lie about a half a kilometre along Minchin Drive, past the sportsground and shopping centre.

THE WINERY RUINS

The remains of the winery complex (ruins may be a better word) can be seen on the corner of Minchin and Barossa drives. Classified as an important piece of industrial archeology, the buildings have nevertheless been partly destroyed by vandals.

Groups of magnificent *Livistona* palms planted in the 1920s still stand here. I counted thirty. These historic palms can be easily spotted from the F4 Western Freeway a couple of hundred metres to the south.

In these days when palm trees can be safely plucked out of the ground by a specially equipped truck, you hope that some benevolent tree lover will move these specimens to a more sympathetic environment—a botanic gardens perhaps. At the moment, surrounded by high fences, they have the look of caged animals.

To be honest, this old complex looks beyond repair, but a more pleasant reminder of the original site lies just across the road. A laneway opposite the intersection of Barossa and Minchin takes you to the Olive Drive. A double row of kalamata olive trees, planted in 1912, lined the original driveway from the highway to the winery. Most of this corridor has been preserved as a kind of green space, although today the trees are enclosed by the back fences of houses and not by rows and rows of grape vines. I counted close to ninety trees so my guess is there were originally a hundred. The drive was obviously designed for horse and cart; there would be no room for trucks or cars to pass each other in opposite directions.

While it is a worthy idea to preserve this narrow slice of history, walking the olive trees can be slightly spooky, almost claustrophobic. The space feels as if it is rarely used by residents, except for those decorating the fences with spray cans. Still, it must be a bonus for locals when the trees bear fruit. The Olive Drive is a couple of hundred metres long and reaches a dead end just after it crosses the northern loop of Minchin Drive and meets the Great Western Highway.

THE PENFOLDS GATES

The concrete bases of the original Penfold's gates, bearing the company name, can still be seen at this point, but these are no longer used and are slowly crumbling away. It looks desolate now but this was once a very grand entrance indeed.

If you want to see how this spot used to look, there is a photo in the nearby McDonald's, about a kilometre to the west on the corner of the Hume Highway and Colyton Road. McDonald's are not usually known as historical museums but this one has several photos of the Minchinbury estate taken in 1909, including one of the original gateway leading to the driveway. At that time, the gates featured an impressive archway with the word 'Minchinbury' spelled out across the top. Will you have fries with that?

THE CIRCULAR HOUSE

This is now a suburb where every house looks pretty much like every other, but in any group there is bound to be one rugged individualist, and here he (or she) is at No. 182 Minchin Drive, just to the east of where the Olive Drive crosses Minchin. Perhaps as a monument to the missing arch over the old Penfold's gates, this house has one across its driveway. But the real treasure is down the back, and the best way to see this is on Gamay Place. In the backyard of No. 182 is a double-storey circular bungalow (as big if not bigger than the main house) with a flat roof that serves as a viewing platform.

This building is clearly visible from the highway (unless they've already built on the spare patch of land behind the house) but I have no idea why this suburban folly was constructed. Astronomy? UFO research? It remains the second Minchinbury mystery, after the great crashing plane debate.

These new suburbs have been designed as democratic entities but in every society there will always be those who want to live a step above everyone else. Even in Minchinbury, there is a luxury district, the local equivalent of Vaucluse. You'll find it by walking back along Minchin Drive, heading west.

Here, on the closest thing to a hill in these flatlands, is a series of comparatively luxurious houses, the kind you are more likely to see in Sylvania Waters. At No. 205 Minchin Drive is a kind of modernised Moorish palace with three lions perched on pillars. In the land of the modern housing estate, the double-storey homeowner is king.

If you follow Minchin Drive down the hill, you'll return to the shopping centre, having walked in a kind of circle. You can finish your modern suburban tour here, or continue westward along the highway, where there is a glimpse of how this area used to be. Those walking Minchinbury should be forewarned that, apart from school kids, few people seem to walk in suburbia. The car rules here.

West from the crashing plane, this highway takes you past Minchinbury Fruit Market, a huge barn selling produce, a modern service station and, on the corner of Archbold Road, the Salvation Army second-hand store, one of Sydney's biggest op shops. This serves as a source of cheap furniture and household goods, but also as a kind of meeting place for locals. It has an outdoor section where piles of books, toys and clothes are literally dumped on trestle tables for people to pick over. As well as locals, inner-city kids come here hoping to find something groovy from the seventies. The inside section features cheap furniture and, oddly, a wide range of antique pianos.

But before suburbia moved in, this area was once full of market gardens and small farms, and one of the few survivors of this era is next to the Salvos. Here is a small property with a hopeful sign advertising 'live chickens, pullets, hens, ducks' for sale. They can also sell you a live goat. Personally, I've never seen anyone drive in to buy one.

WALKING
POINT
PIPER

SUMMARY: *A circular walk takes you down the most expensive street in Australia, according to Sydney's real estate agents, taking in the beautiful Redleaf Pool, a stroll along exclusive Seven Shillings Beach (where an invisible line in the sand separates the public and private sections) ending at the celebrity-concious Police Station on the corner of Wunulla Road, set in an historic gatekeeper's lodge.*
START AND FINISH: *New South Head Road; Sydney Buses 323 – 325.*
LENGTH: *One and a half kilometres.*
TIME: *One and a half hours.*
REFRESHMENTS: *Food and coffee at the Redleaf Pool kiosk, a wide choice of restaurants and pubs at nearby Double Bay.*

POINT
PIPER

FELIX BAY

ROSE BAY

DOUBLE BAY

BLACKBURN COVE

WOOLLAHRA POINT

POINT PIPER

LADY MARTINS BEACH

DUFF PARK

ROSE PARK

NEW SOUTH HEAD RD

ROSE BAY AV

VICTORIA RD

NEW SOUTH HEAD RD

BUCKHURST AV

ST MERVYNS AV

SEVEN SHILLINGS BEACH

WINGADAL PL

WENTWORTH ST

WYUNA RD

WUNULLA RD

WOLSELEY RD

LONGWORTH AV

START

70

A
ccording to Sydney's real estate agents, Point Piper is the most exclusive suburb in Australia, and Wolseley Road is the most expensive address. It's hard to see the attraction of these places from the footpath, because all you can see are high fences and locked garage doors. There are occasional glimpses of water but if you want to see what people are prepared to pay ten million dollars to look at from their balconies, you can see the same thing on Seven Shillings Beach for absolutely nothing.

REDLEAF POOL

The best way in to Seven Shillings is via Redleaf Pool. There's a gateway and ramp leading down from New South Head Road opposite the intersection with Victoria Road. The building just to your right is Woollahra Municipal Library, surely the best location for a library in Sydney. The only problem is that the stunning views over the harbour make it very difficult to concentrate on the written word.

Immediately below the library are Blackburn Gardens, small, formal and beautifully restored to maintain the period setting, including a sundial in the centre of the lawn. A gate at the bottom of these gardens opens onto the driveway which takes you past a handball court and into the terrace above the recently restored Redleaf Pool.

Surprisingly for such an exclusive area, the public can swim here for nothing. Redleaf is the nearest harbour pool to the CBD, enclosed by sharkproof netting and a circular boardwalk placed high above the water for diving. Two pontoons are placed in the middle of what, usually, is clean salt water (but best to wait a few days after heavy rain). A cafe with surprisingly good food, and excellent coffee, overlooks the pool. The general atmosphere is more Italian Riviera than Eastern Suburbs.

SEVEN SHILLINGS BEACH

For most, Redleaf is a perfect place to spend all day, but for to see how the other half lives, there's a gateway to Seven Shillings Beach on the right hand side. You enter at your own risk. The beach at the bottom of the most expensive street in Sydney is only partially open to the public. A sign here, and others placed along the beach, say that access is only allowed 'below the mean high water mark'. The beach above the mean high water mark belongs to the very rich people who own the adjoining properties.

Exactly where this theoretical line in the sand is drawn is not clear, but the message is that you are not entirely welcome here. In fact, some of the houses feature barbed wire along the tops of their fences.

There is a long-running history of disputes between landowners and the council to have this beach closed to the public. So far, the council has kept the beach open to the public and the mean high water mark, apparently, is someone's idea of a compromise. Another compromise is the shutting of the gates allowing public access between sunset and sunrise.

Once you make it onto the sacred sand (above the mean high water mark naturally), you may wonder what all the fuss is about. Seven Shillings, sad to say, is less than spectacular. The sand is dirty, the surf is non-existent and this particular section appears to be a natural trap for much of the rubbish that thoughtless people on boats toss into the harbour. Few people swim here. Residents certainly don't. They have private pools, of course.

The most famous resident of Seven Shillings Beach is Lady Mary Fairfax. If you're lucky, you may bump into her walking her Doberman. Regular visitors have experienced her sumptuous garden parties from the beach, where her black tie A-list guests nibble hors d'oeuvres oblivious to the fact that, just over the wall, semi-naked strangers are sunbathing on her beach.

It's interesting to note that even Point Piper is not immune to graffiti attacks and Mary Fairfax's front fence is a popular target for taggers.

THE CHINESE BOATHOUSE

But there is good reason to impose further upon the good lady's privacy. About two hundred metres north along Seven Shillings Beach is one of Sydney's most delightful architectural curiosities, a Chinoiserie boathouse. Painted turquoise and beautifully maintained, this building can normally only be seen from the water. It comes with the adjoining mansion, but even on its own, it would be worth more than a couple of complete suburban homes. For those living on the harbour, a boatshed is an important status symbol and this one beats all others, except maybe for the one around the corner that was converted into a floating helipad.

A local story, which may or may not be an urban myth, concerns the previous owners of this boathouse who wanted to moor their very large yacht close by. The water around here is not very deep so they decided to dredge a channel leading directly to the boathouse. Unfortunately this had an unpleasant side-effect. Every time they dredged, the already narrow strip of exposed sand on the beach completely disappeared. After numerous complaints, they were forced to moor their big boat elsewhere.

The beach is also notorious for, of all things, drug smuggling. A well-remembered drug dealer used to live in an old ferry just off this beach and it was a source of much local amusement to watch desperate young people paddling out in an assortment of small craft to obtain supplies.

The boathouse marks the end of public access to the beach, so if you want to see more of how the rich live, it's back down St Mervyns Lane (between sunrise and sunset only) and left at Wolseley Road.

But back to the contentious issue. A sign in the laneway attempts to define the mysterious mean high water mark. At this point, it's five metres from the fenceline, so you'll have to walk further out than that. At another part of the beach, another sign indicates it's eleven metres out. By my calculations, at certain times of the day and the year (especially in dredging season), you'd be walking waist-deep in water to keep yourself legal.

If it all sounds like a Monty Python sketch, you're right. They may be rich but they're also very silly.

THE AMAZING CAPTAIN PIPER

Blame it, perhaps, on Captain Piper, the colonial Collector of Customs after whom this suburb is named. He started a very silly tradition. A dandy and spendthrift who eventually went bankrupt, Piper's chief claim to fame was his faked suicide attempt. He did this, in impeccable style, by having his servants row him out into the harbour where he threw himself overboard with a flourish. They promptly rescued him and rowed him to shore.

Back to Wolseley Road, that most expensive address in Australia. But only one side of the street. Veering left past Buckhurst Avenue, the houses on your left are those with, in real estate speak, 'absolute water frontage'. You can expect to pay at least a million dollars more for these three magic words.

DUFF RESERVE

If you want to experience what you get for that million dollars more, you can see for yourself at a gateway between Nos. 130 and 132.

At the bottom of a steep flight of stairs is Duff Reserve, a small island of weedy grass, strewn with discarded wine casks when I last visited. But this is 'absolute water frontage' so, according to current market prices, what am I bid? In fact this is a public park, so it's yours for nothing.

It's one of Sydney's ironies that a homeless person can spend the day here, sitting in the shade of the rotunda with a cask of wine, enjoying much the same views of the Harbour Bridge as the filthy rich person in the multi-million dollar house a couple of metres away.

This is a street full of ironies. If you walk Wolseley Road during the week you will notice that, instead of the Rolls Royces and Porsches you might expect to see, most of the cars in this street are muddy and battered utes.

There's an explanation. These are tradesmen's vehicles. At dawn, a small army of builders and swimming pool cleaners arrive to work at what appears to be a continual process of renovation.

There is also the noticeable presence of security persons, either updating the burglar-resistance of properties, or simply standing outside, perhaps making sure that the tradesmen don't leave with more than they entered. During a walk, it is rare to see anyone who looks like they actually live here. Much more likely to be the nanny, the dog walker or the personal trainer. Or the private detective, checking up on who is being personally trained.

Although several titled people live in this street, this is nothing to get too excited about. In Australia, people with titles are treated more with suspicion than reverence. Sir Les Patterson (whose creator, Barry Humphries, owns a place not too far away) is not considered such a huge exaggeration. This street is not without its sense of humour. A brass plaque on the gate at No. 138 Wolseley Road bears the message, 'Never mind the dog, beware of the owner'.

To return to New South Head Road, you turn right at Wyuna Road which, after a couple of hundred metres, merges with Wunulla Road. This road was once the tree-lined driveway leading up to Woollahra House, built here in 1883 by William Cooper. It's interesting to work out what Cooper's entire estate, which covered much of the suburb, would be worth these days. Probably more than the rest of Australia put together.

Woollahra House was sold in 1899 to an English syndicate who resold it, needless to say, for a handsome profit. The house was demolished in 1929 and the estate subdivided but two of the original buildings remain. One is a block of flats at No. 1a Wyuna Road, now called Wyuna Court. These were originally the stables.

SYDNEY'S STRANGEST POLICE STATION

At the bottom of Wunulla Road, on the corner of New South Head Road, lies the second remnant of the Woollahra estate. This building is perhaps the quaintest police station in Sydney. It used to be the gatekeeper's lodge.

Rose Bay Police Station, now painted in sympathetic heritage colours, is the cop shop of choice for celebrities, where the officers are trained in discretion as well as detection. It was from here that the police were called over to investigate the death of rock singer Michael Hutchence when he suicided at the nearby Ritz Carlton hotel.

They are well-trained in diplomacy at the Rose Bay gatekeeper's lodge. When interviewed by the media, the officer-in-charge politely refused to even divulge the name of his most recent client. It was a performance worthy of a veteran publicist.

Perhaps it's because Wunulla Road has such a star-studded history. Just a hundred metres north of the station, next to the Royal Motor Yacht Club, is the former home of Nellie Stewart. Sweet Nell was Australia's most famous actress around the turn of the century, although she kept on performing until she died in 1931. Her house was called Den O'Gwynn after her most famous stage role as Nell Gwynne.

Would Nell have minded strangers walking below the mean high water mark on her beach? Of course not, she loved her public.

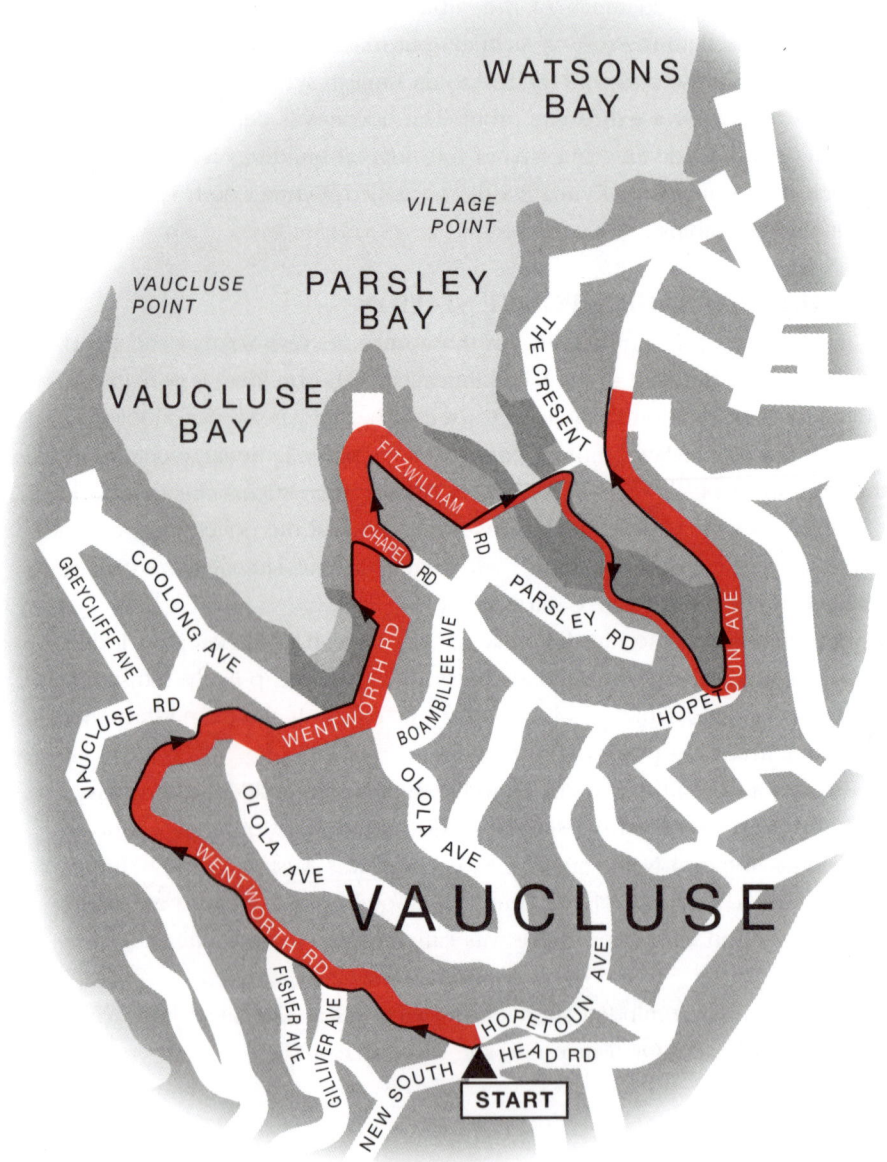

WATSONS
BAY

VILLAGE
POINT

VAUCLUSE
POINT

PARSLEY
BAY

VAUCLUSE
BAY

THE CRESENT

FITZWILLIAM

CHAPEL RD

RD

PARSLEY RD

HOPETOUN AVE

GREYCLIFFE AVE

COOLONG AVE

VAUCLUSE RD

WENTWORTH RD

BOAMBILLEE AVE

OLOLA AVE

OLOLA AVE

VAUCLUSE

WENTWORTH RD

FISHER AVE

GILLIVER AVE

NEW SOUTH

HOPETOUN AVE

HEAD RD

HOPETOUN AVE

START

Walking

Vaucluse

SUMMARY: *This is a walk, mostly downhill, that passes through the mansion-lined streets of Vaucluse, takes in a working lighthouse in a front garden, a mausoleum hidden in a suburban street and, at the end of an alleyway, a suspension bridge over one of Sydney's most secluded and beautiful bays. Here, in a small pocket off bush just a few kilometres from the CBD, you may be lucky enough to see a real dragon sunbaking on a rock. There is no admission fee to Parsley Bay Reserve.*

START: *Corner of Wentworth Road and Hopetoun Avenue; Sydney Bus 324 or 325. To get to Vaucluse from the city, take the Watsons Bay via the Vaucluse Heights bus to Stop 06.*

FINISH: *Corner Hopetoun Avenue and the Crescent (Sydney Bus 325, or a short walk along Hopetoun to Watsons Bay ferry).*

LENGTH: *Two kilometres.*

TIME: *One and a half hours.*

REFRESHMENTS: *Snacks at Parsley Bay Reserve kiosk; pubs and restaurants at Watsons Bay.*

T his suburb may be where the seriously rich people live, but there is also history to be freely seen, and some unexpected treasures as well. The best place to start is from the bus stop on Hopetoun Avenue, just after it diverges left from New South Head Road. History greets you as soon as you step off the bus. The dark green wooden hut is one of the few remaining tram shelters in Sydney. To the chagrin of many, the Sydney tram system was axed in the early 1960s. The Watsons Bay run was the pride of the system but this is about all that's left.

ON TOP OF HEARTBREAK HILL

You'll be pleased to note that the bus has taken you to the top of what competitors in the annual City to Surf fun run dread most—Heartbreak Hill. The slope seems innocuous enough until you try to climb it on foot. The good news is that it's (mostly) downhill from here.

Wentworth Road, immediately adjacent the bus/tram stop, curves gently downhill past some of Sydney's finest and oldest mansions. You can practically smell the money as you walk past. Here are houses owned by, among other celebrities, filmmaker Jane Campion. Hers is the house that *The Piano* bought.

LIGHTHOUSE FOR PIXIES

But there are less expensive treasures as well. At No. 12 is a tiny white and blue lighthouse on the front lawn, looking as if it was built for pixies. When I was first shown this building, I thought it must be a folly, constructed last century by some eccentric retired sea dog. The truth is slightly less romantic. This is a functional harbour marker (rear leading light marker, to be technical), one of two used to define the Eastern Channel of Port Jackson.

Despite its distance from the water (which can't be seen from ground level) this light can easily be seen by ships on the harbour. The lighthouse is in the grounds of what is now the Canadian Embassy, but it has its own small landscaped garden and front gate and is independently connected to street electricity. It's especially beautiful at night.

There are many houses of architectural interest along Wentworth Road, but a slight detour left at Gilliver Avenue takes you to one of Sydney's finest examples of the Spanish mission style. The mansion at No. 19, complete with a turret and fading paint, is a rare original and unrestored survivor of the style that was also popular in Hollywood in the 1920s and 1930s. You can easily imagine Bogie and Bacall stepping out of this front door.

THE WENTWORTH MAUSOLEUM

Wentworth Road takes you directly past the front gates of Vaucluse House, a place so popular as to be hardly worthy of a mention in a book about Sydney's secrets. But it too has its secrets, and one of those is Wentworth Mausoleum. It's no longer part of the Vaucluse House grounds, but two streets further along Wentworth Road, in Chapel Road.

As you walk this street, you may notice an absence of snakes. This is because Sir Henry Browne Hayes, the former sheriff of County Cork who first built Vaucluse House (it was later taken over by the statesman and explorer William Charles Wentworth) constructed a moat around his estate filled, not with water, but with 500 barrels of soil imported especially from snake-free Ireland. It must have worked. These days snakes are pretty rare in Vaucluse, although chances are you'll see some dragons further along.

The lasting symbol of Wentworth's eccentricity is his mausoleum in Chapel Road. This is surely one of Sydney's most surreal buildings, all the more so because today it is situated in a perfectly normal residential street.

The story goes that Wentworth, who was granted most of this land after his successful explorations of the Blue Mountains, liked to sit on this spot to look out over the harbour. He requested he be placed in a mausoleum here, and they carried out his wishes literally. The mausoleum is perched on a large sandstone boulder, a concept that today would be termed post-modern. In 1873, when it was built, it must have shocked and amazed.

Even on a sunny summer's day, the Wentworth mausoleum seems to be surrounded by a time capsule of gothic gloom. If you walk up behind the chapel, you can see Wentworth's coffin placed on the spot of his choice.

Back to Wentworth Road and two more surprises for pedestrians. On the corner of Wentworth and Fitzwilliam Roads is a flagpole and two ancient cannons, erected here in 1918 as 'a grateful tribute to the gallant men who fought for us in the Great War'. A few metres further along is Sydney's only grotto bus shelter, in front of the Airthrey estate. My guess is the grotto was here well before the buses arrived on the scene, but when they did, someone with a sense of humour snapped it up. Unfortunately, like every other bus shelter, grotto or not, it has been vandalised by graffiti gangs.

Another unexpected surprise, and this is a big one, is a hundred metres away down Fitzwilliam, just before it intersects with Parsley Road. Near the bus stop on your left is a laneway signposted 'To Parsley Bay Reserve'.

THE SUSPENSION BRIDGE

If you walk along this path, you will soon find yourself standing on an old suspension bridge stretching across one of Sydney's most spectacular natural beaches. It can take your breath away, and not only because the bridge tends to vibrate when you walk upon it.

Probably because so few people seem to know about it, Parsley Bay remains one of Sydney's greatest treasures. This enclosed area still retains the atmosphere of the Edwardian era when it was best known for Sunday School picnics. The graceful suspension bridge, designed by Edwin Sautelle, dates back to 1910, when it was originally used to transport people across the bay to a long-gone ferry stop on the wharf.

Other vintage touches at Parsley Bay include the house and kiosk on the lawns, built circa 1920 and occupied by a very lucky ranger, and a curious engraved rock near where the public toilets stand today. Next to a series of steps leading up to what used to be a small kiosk, this boulder has been carved, a long time ago, with the words 'lunch, costumes, boiling water'— in other words, a sandstone billboard.

To enter Parsley Bay (either by the walkway leading to the bridge, or by Horler Avenue, the lane towards the end of Parsley Road which leads to a small car park) is to step back five decades or more.

Apart from summer weekends, the park appears to be rarely used except by the locals who swim across its clear, shark-proof waters. At the mouth of the bay, a shark net achieves what the ditch of Irish soil does at Vaucluse House. On the other side of the bridge is a shallow sandy beach which is safe for children. There are large areas of lawn and barbeque facilities. This is one of the best spots in Sydney for a picnic.

THE BONSAI FIG

One of the secret joys of Parsley Bay is best seen by swimming the fifty metres across the mouth of the bay, following the line of the shark net, to the small aluminium ladder on the western corner. Just above the ladder on a rock ledge is a small gnarled fig tree that has somehow grown out of a crevice just a few metres above water level. A natural bonsai, the fig is less than a metre tall although, judging by the bark, it has been there a long time. My amateur guess is thirty years at least. The tree seems to be thriving in the damp, salty air and enjoying the panoramic harbour views. How they grow out of solid rock is one of nature's miracles.

If you can't swim across, you can visit the tree at low tide by rock-hopping along the western edge of the pool. This is a shoes-only trip. The rock shelves here are encrusted with oyster shells, but it's worth the effort.

Just past the bonsai fig stands a faded white obelisk next to a pink boatshed. This is not, as it would appear, some nineteenth-century memorial, but another navigational aid. The line between this obelisk and the stone cairn standing on Laings Point at Watsons Bay marks the western extreme of South Reef. These markers have now been replaced by a flashing light beacon.

HOME OF THE EASTERN WATER DRAGON

At the other end of Parsley Bay is a nature reserve, with an uphill pathway winding through a small patch of rainforest. Access is from the car park. In wet weather, a small creek runs freely through this reserve, complete with waterfalls. Despite being surrounded by a residential area, this sliver of wilderness is home to a group of eastern water dragons (*Physignathus lesueri*), grey and black striped lizards that can be a metre long when fully mature. There are thought to be as many as a hundred of these dragons living in this small space. They are frequently seen sunbaking by the creek in summer. Their main threat is the domestic cat.

The existence of dragons is not the only natural surprise in these parts. As recently as 1966, naturalists were startled to find the body of an eastern quoll (*Dasyurus viverrinus*) run over by a car on the road next to Nielsen Park, just a hundred metres from Vaucluse House.

Tragically, this was the last recorded sighting of this beautifully marked mammal on the mainland. Incredible as it may sound, the last survivors of the species had been living just ten kilometres from the centre of Australia's most populated city, in a small area of parkland packed on the weekends with swimmers and picnickers. The last Nielsen Park quoll is now a prized preserved specimen at the Australian Museum. You can't help wondering if the driver of that fateful car ever realised that he or she was accidentally responsible for making a species extinct.

'Now, rather than making a small trip into inner Sydney to see this beautiful species, we must travel to Tasmania, its only remaining refuge,' wrote the Australian Museum's Dr Tim Flannery. The quolls may be gone but at least you can still see dragons at Parsley Bay.

The pathway through the nature reserve takes you back (up some steep steps) to Hopetoun Avenue, with easy access to buses to the City or Watsons Bay. The trouble, of course, in having found this magic place, is forcing yourself to leave. This is especially tricky for those with cars. The park gates close at sunset and to have the gates opened after then will cost you $20, but only 'if the ranger is home' according to the proviso on the sign.

Fans of historic navigational markers may like to see another ancient obelisk which is only visible from Sassafras Lane, the alley running between The Crescent and Hopetoun Avenue. While no longer in use, the owners of the property in which it stands are proud of this curiosity in their backyard.

At least four metres tall, it has been boldly decorated with red and white triangles which gives it the surreal appearance of something out of a Jeffrey Smart painting. The owners have tried to research the history of the obelisk and have even produced a fact sheet to give to friends or, in my case, total strangers taking photos over their back fence.

According to their research, the obelisk was built around 1836 when it was first shown in local plans. When lined up with the Macquarie Lighthouse, it defines the southern edge of the Sow and Pigs Reef. The word 'Wreath' is engraved at the base of the structure, but the meaning of this remains a mystery. To quote from the fact sheet: 'the Mitchell Library research officer has no further information and the Maritime Services Board is hopeless'.

WALKING
WATSONS
BAY

SUMMARY: *A walk through the significant history of Watsons Bay, from the infamous Gap, scene of countless suicide attempts, brings you to the cemetery on Old South Head Road, where you'll find the Packer family vault. Perched on the cliffs overlooking the Tasman Sea is one of Australia's most spectacular churches, a few metres from the place where the First Fleet landed, camping overnight before deciding to plant their flag a few kilometres further down Port Jackson. Later this site had a different claim to fame, becoming the first legal topless beach in Australia.*
START: *The Gap Park, Military Road (Sydney Buses 325 or 324, or take the Watsons Bay ferry from Wharf 4, Circular Quay).*
FINISH: *South Head Cemetery, Old South Head Road (Sydney Buses 387 or, on New South Head Road, 324).*
LENGTH: *Three kilometres, including some medium hills.*
TIME: *Three hours.*
REFRESHMENTS: *Several pubs, restaurants and milk bars throughout Watsons Bay, including the famous Doyle's seafood restaurant near the ferry wharf.*

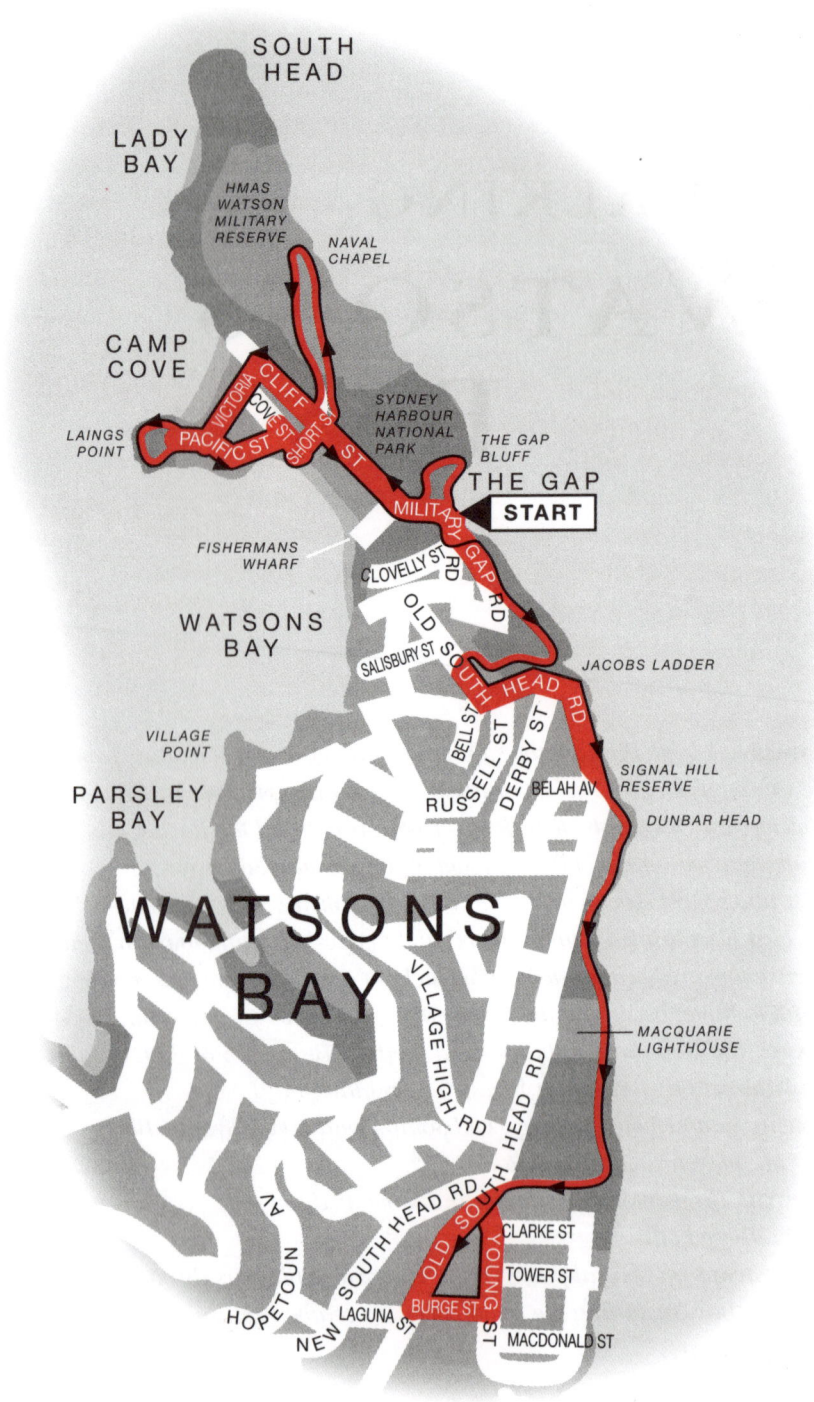

SOUTH
HEAD

LADY
BAY

HMAS
WATSON
MILITARY
RESERVE

NAVAL
CHAPEL

CAMP
COVE

SYDNEY
HARBOUR
NATIONAL
PARK

THE GAP
BLUFF

LAINGS
POINT

CLIFF ST

VICTORIA ST

COVE ST

SHORT ST

PACIFIC ST

THE GAP

MILITARY GAP RD

START

FISHERMANS
WHARF

CLOVELLY ST RD

JACOBS LADDER

WATSONS
BAY

OLD SOUTH HEAD RD

SALISBURY ST

OLD SOUTH HEAD RD

VILLAGE
POINT

BELL ST

RUSSELL ST

DERBY ST

BELAH AV

SIGNAL HILL
RESERVE

PARSLEY
BAY

DUNBAR HEAD

WATSONS
BAY

VILLAGE HIGH RD

MACQUARIE
LIGHTHOUSE

OLD SOUTH HEAD RD

AV

HOPETOUN

NEW SOUTH HEAD RD

LAGUNA ST

BURGE ST

YOUNG ST

CLARKE ST

TOWER ST

MACDONALD ST

I t may be a beautiful location, but it does have its darker side. All around this narrow peninsula is evidence of shipwrecks, death and war. Something to chat about while you wait for your 'fisherman's basket' at Doyle's. The cliffs on the eastern side of Watsons Bay, known as the Gap, are the big attraction. Here waves that formed in New Zealand waters pound against the rocks. Even those who don't believe in the supernatural feel that there is something elemental about the place. Maybe it's because so many have died here.

THE INFAMOUS GAP

The Gap is best known as Sydney's favourite suicide spot. This fact is cheerfully promoted on postcards. 'Renowned for its extreme steepness of cliffs, which are often chosen for suicide attempts,' claims one. All that's missing is an arrow and the words, 'jump here'.

Most treat it as a joke. When Alfred Hitchcock visited Sydney in 1960 to promote his movie *Psycho*, the world's most famous ghoul insisted on being photographed perched on the railing, as if about to dive.

Today's visitors to the Gap arrive by the busload. I'm not sure whether the hordes of smiling Japanese, taking a three-second photo opportunity, realise the social significance of the place. Still, it's rare to visit without seeing at least one practical joker doing a Hitch by pretending to hurdle the fence. Tragedy has a habit of happening here.

THE WRECK OF THE *DUNBAR*

The anchor from the *Dunbar*, the most famous of several ships to be wrecked near this spot, is placed against a rock wall. It's a stark reminder of a bitterly cold night in 1857 when 121 people died. Only one survived. The wreck of the *Dunbar* is the closest Australia has to the *Titanic* disaster, and this amazing story unfolds, chapter by chapter, as you walk south along the cliffs.

REXIE THE WONDER DOG

But the Gap is also a place for heroes. And one of the greatest wasn't even human. According to legend, Rexie, a female German Shepherd, saved over thirty lives in the 1960s by sniffing out potential suicides and alerting her owner, John Nagy. Once, according to an ABC TV report, Rexie got too close to a man about to jump. He grabbed her collar. Nagy ran over.

'I said to him, "Please, please, you go but leave the dog, don't take the dog with you." So he let go the dog,' Nagy told the reporter, adding that from that day on Rexie never wore a collar.

John Nagy owned the Gap Tavern, a mock-Tudor restaurant that stood, until recently, on the end of Gap Road nearest to the steps leading up to the cliff. At the height of her fame, Rexie's portrait was featured on a sign swinging English pub-style above the front door. Thanks to the gimmick of the hero dog, the Gap Tavern became a celebrity hangout. Irish comedian Dave Allen was a regular visitor.

Today there are signs at the Gap saying 'Dogs Totally Prohibited. Maximum Penalty $500'. Rexie the wonder dog would be costing her owner a fortune these days. Plus extra for having no collar.

It's a pity there is no monument to Rexie. Even the locals now need prompting to remember her name. The Gap Tavern has been replaced by a spectacular new building that is as futuristic as the previous one was quaint.

POLICE RESCUE

The best-known human hero of the Gap was Special Sergeant Harry Ware, the man who founded the NSW Police Rescue Squad. Ware was nick-named 'the rock spider' due to his phenomenal climbing skills. It was he who had the unpleasant task of rescuing the dead bodies of those who jumped from the Gap, as well as the still living bodies of fishermen who tried to climb down the cliffs. He became a folk hero, rating a mention in Les Murray's poem, 'The Breach':

'I said to Ware once, "Harry, you're the best cop of the lot: you only arrest falls." He was amused'.

Ware died in 1970, of natural causes. His ashes were scattered in the waters off the Gap while the Police Rescue Squad formed a guard of honour along the fence. As if out of respect, the waters were unusually calm that day. The squad which he founded was to become the inspiration for the very popular *Police Rescue* television series.

1. Lyall Randolph, the Leonardo
da Vinci of Bondi, hard at work
creating one of his mermaids.
2. Ten years later, on the rocks
at Ben Buckler.

3. *Sadly, no more. The crumbling remains of the Star of the East Amphitheatre, Balmoral Beach.*

4. *Here lies Granny Smith.*

5. The King of Castlecrag, Leonard Teale, in his 'Homicide' days.

On the corner of Hunter and Castlereagh Streets, Sydney, the P. & O. Shipping Line has completed its contribution to the Australian Calico scene—the P. & O. Building, officially opened by the Prime Minister in January. To alleviate the scene drabness of its ambitious facade, sculptor Tom Bass has set an attractive bronze urinal in the wall for the convenience of passersby. This is no ordinary urinal. It has a sculptural flushing system and basins handily set at different standing heights. There is a nominal charge, of course, but don't worry, there is no need to pay immediately.   Just P. & O. Pictured is a trio of Sydney natives P. & O'ing in the Bass urinal.

6. You mean it isn't a urinal? Three teenagers do the obvious at the Tom Bass fountain, as depicted on the cover of Oz magazine.

7. Casa Clavel, the moorish mansion of Sydney's original flamboyant medico, Dr Reginald Stuart-Jones, is in Bellevue Hill.

8. Wentworth's mausoleum, perched on his favourite rock near Parsley Bay.

9. One of the prize exhibits in Joe Ferla's mad monster garden.

10. Driving onwards forever. The gravestone of racing driver Phil Garlick at South Head Cemetery.

11. Murals by artist Arthur Barton line the inside walls of Luna Park's Coney Island.

12. A ghost of its former self. Luna Park, when it was having fun.

13. The witch of Kings Cross, Rosaleen Norton, at her Kings Cross coven.

Despite the best efforts of Rexie and Harry Ware, it has almost become a Sydney tradition to end your life at the Gap, notably with high-profile people. In 1991, Mary Jane Boyd, a forty-year-old singer who had featured regularly on television in the 1970s, ended her life by jumping.

To look down is to wonder why. Pills must be much more pleasant. But as John Nagy said more than twenty years before, famous people choose the Gap because that way they are guaranteed some final media coverage.

For those who come here to look and not to jump, there is still plenty of excitement. A walk north along the cliffs to Gap Bluff takes you up to one of the highest vantage points. But for locals this spot had a much more ignominious claim to fame. Here, on the edge of the world, was where the famous Gap Dunny stood. Its ruins were only recently removed. It must have been one of the oldest public conveniences in Sydney.

'When it was erected is anyone's guess but, if it was not before Vaucluse Council was inaugurated in 1895, it would have been one of Council's first projects,' writes local historian Jack Woodward. Instead of a modern water flush system, the Gap Dunny allowed gravity to do the job. Waste was delivered directly to the rocks and water below. It is still possible to see the channel in the rock which fed sewage directly over the cliff.

Also at this point are the remaining buildings belonging to the School of Artillery, which was based here from 1894 to the start of World War II. The old officers' mess building, built in 1936 in the P&O 'ocean liner' style, is now used as a convention centre. The public is free to look around this area. Another rare building is the toilet block, dating from 1912, with an obviously well-fertilised palm tree growing next to it.

THE CHAPEL ON THE CLIFFS

There are several influences of the armed services at Watsons Bay, and the most obvious of these is the HMAS Watsons Bay Reserve at the end of Cliff Street. Although still an operational base, the public is allowed in to see the remarkable Naval Chapel perched on the edge of the cliffs at South Head. Opened in 1961, the chapel on the cliffs is noted for the inspiring views of the heads through its floor-to-ceiling east window. Here stained glass is relegated to the side walls.

Most of the fittings have been donated by overseas navies. The lectern, in the shape of a kea bird with wings spread, was carved by a craftsman from Auckland Naval Dockyard. The altar features a mosaic of stones donated by thirty-three cathedrals and churches from around the world. A booklet is available for a $4 donation.

The church with the best views in Sydney is open to the public daily between 8am and 4pm (except Christmas Day and Boxing Day). The public is welcome to attend Sunday Mass at 9am. As you walk up to the chapel, you will be reminded of the real purpose of HMAS Watsons Bay. A selection of historic weapons, including an anti-submarine missile, are displayed by the side of the road.

For those interested in naval history, the next port of call is up Cliff Street, then left at Victoria and right at Pacific to Camp Cove. The section of Cliff Street near the entrance to the naval base is well-known for its four original fishing cottages. There are few left now, but once this suburb was full of these tiny wooden shacks.

CAMP COVE

Camp Cove is famous for two reasons. There is a marker on the steps leading down to the sand which records that this, and not Sydney Cove, was the first landing place of Governor Phillip and the First Fleet in 1788. On January 21st they landed offshore and camped here overnight. But it wasn't until five days later, Australia Day, that he returned to Port Jackson and unfurled his flag a few kilometres further down. If he hadn't, Watsons Bay may now be Sydney's CBD.

Camp Cove's other claim to fame is that it was Australia's first topless beach. The next beach north, Lady Bay, goes one step further and is completely nude.

Laings Point, the headland immediately to the left of Camp Cove, is one of the former anchor points of the World War II submarine net that stretched across the harbour to Middle Head. This net had a gate that allowed ships to pass through. Despite the incredible expense of this barrier, two of the three Japanese midget subs that invaded Sydney also sneaked through. All that remains of the net on Laings Point are the foundations of a winching hut.

THE BOER WAR MEMORIAL

There is more naval history to be explored along the cliff path to the south of the the Gap. Along the way is a rare military interruption. The Boer War memorial, dedicated to Lieutenant G. T. Grieve, who fell at the battle of Paardeberg in 1900, is placed on the cliffs at the southern end of the Gap Park, near the chasm in the rock wall known as Jacob's Ladder. Jimmie Grieve was a local boy who lived in Old South Head Road directly opposite his memorial.

At this point, a detour up Old South Head Road takes you to historic St Peters church, designed by Edmund Blacket in 1846. Last century it was known as the Pilots Church because it was the first and last landmark for sailors entering and leaving the harbour. No doubt many a silent prayer was said in its direction on stormy nights.

THE *GREYCLIFFE* DISASTER

On the entrance gates to St Peters is a reminder of yet another shipwreck, the *Greycliffe* disaster of 1927. This was not a result of a storm. This was the result of a nautical traffic jam.

By the 1920s, Sydney Harbour, which Governor Phillip had found empty 130 years before, had become one of the busiest harbours in the world.

In the days before radar, disaster was waiting to happen. It did with a bang when the ferry *Greycliffe* was hit by the steamer *Tahiti* off Bradleys Head. The wooden ferry was sliced in two by the 7,000-tonne ship. Forty died, many of them children on their way home from school.

Behind St Peters lies a small, secret garden of remembrance, where the ashes of 'any person regardless of residence or religion' may be kept. The garden winds like a maze beneath sandstone overhangs. Water drips into a small pond. It is a beautiful place to visit, but for those on the move, stage two of the Dunbar story awaits us up the hill.

While the ship's anchor is placed at the Gap, the *Dunbar* was actually wrecked a little to the south. The exact spot is directly opposite the house at No. 248 Old South Head Road. A modern plaque has been placed against the fence overlooking the cliff, but a more romantic memorial is the engraving in the rocks just a few metres to the north.

This can be easily seen from the safe side of the fence. It reads 'DUNBAR. CP 25th August 1857'. The more recent comment 'recut 20 August 1906 by ESS' is a reference to Vaucluse Town Clerk Edwin Sautelle, who organised the recutting of the original carvings. Down below is where the *Dunbar* hit the cliffs around midnight. Looking down, it is easy to see why only one person survived.

THE SAGA OF JAMES JOHNSON

At this point, spare a thought for that one survivor. James Johnson somehow managed to jump overboard and scramble onto a narrow ledge. Here he remained for thirty-six hours, freezing and starving, waiting to be rescued. It's easy to imagine that there must have been times when he would have preferred to drown than be where he was, even when found he faced a perilous journey up the cliff on the end of a rope.

These days Johnson would be snapped up by Harry M. Miller and paid a fortune (less 25 per cent commission) to tell his story exclusively on '60 Minutes'. Before the age of television, Johnson's reward, ironically, was to be appointed a lighthouse keeper. In 1858, he became the first keeper at the new Hornby Lighthouse on inner South Head, just a few hundred metres north of where he came to grief. Hornby was built after yet another shipwreck, the *Catherine Adamson*, occurred just two months after the *Dunbar*.

At times Johnson must have suffered from considerable 'deja vu'. In 1866 he was employed at Newcastle Lighthouse when the steamship *Cawarra* was wrecked on Oyster Bank. There was only one survivor, Frederick Hedges. One guess who managed to pull Hedges from the water. There are even more stories of the *Dunbar* as we travel south.

But first, there are more reminders of World War II. At the entry to Signal Hill Reserve are the remains of various gun emplacements and the dark entrances to some tunnels. These were used during the defence of Sydney but they now have a rather sinister appearance. Some graffiti on a door sums up the atmosphere: 'Dead Ghosts—don't go inside, you won't come out alive'. The metal doors leading down to the ghostly homes are permanently shut.

FRANCIS GREENWAY'S LIGHTHOUSE

From here the cliff walk takes you past two prominent structures, the Signal Station and the Macquarie Lighthouse. The Signal Station celebrated its bicentenary in 1990, making it, according to Roy Davies, the resident signalmaster, 'the longest continually manned site in Australia'. It began as a lookout in 1790, where sailors scanned the ocean for twelve days at a time. It was also the site of Australia's first navigational beacon, a large wood fire. Macquarie Lighthouse, a short distance south, then took over this role.

Many people take great pleasure in looking at lighthouses (me, for starters) but this one is literally a symbol of freedom. The current structure is a direct copy of the original building designed by convict architect Francis Greenway. When the lighthouse was nearly completed in 1818, Governor Macquarie rode out to inspect the work and, over breakfast, granted Greenway a conditional pardon.

After the sandstone began to crumble, the original lighthouse was replaced by the existing version in 1883. They must have found some A-grade sandstone this time.

By the way, the row of flats next to the lighthouse are sometimes available to the public for rent. Nice views—but you have to keep the blinds down at night if you want to sleep. The walk south past the lighthouse takes you through Christison Park to South Head Cemetery on the corner of Old South Head Road and Young Street.

SOUTH HEAD CEMETERY

The *Dunbar* saga, part three. Here lies the gravestone (a fouled anchor, carved from marble) of Captain James Green. While the other victims of the tragedy were buried in a mass grave at St Stephens, in Camperdown, the captain was buried here, not far from the scene of the disaster. Despite miscalculating the entrance to the harbour by a kilometre or so, Green was absolved of any direct blame. At the inquest into the loss of the ship (Lucky Jim Johnson was the star witness), the jury's verdict was reported as, 'There may have been an error of judgement in the vessel being so close to the shore at night in such bad weather, but they do not attach any blame to Captain Green or his officers for the loss of the ship'.

Captain Green's grave is not the most photographed in this cemetery, for South Head features one of the most celebrated gravestones in Australia.

In 1926, Phil Garlick was one of Australia's first motorsports heroes when he lost his life by crashing at the infamous Maroubra Speedway. He was driving an Alvis with the dreaded number thirteen on the tail. The car was called 'Lucky Devil'. After more fatalities, the Maroubra 'killer track' was closed and demolished. This South Head memorial, featuring a life-size statue of flying Phil at the wheel, is one of the few reminders of the track's existence.

Another feature of the cemetery is the Packer Mausoleum, the eventual resting place of Australia's richest man, Kerry Packer. There's nothing fancy about this structure. Like the man it will one day contain, this is solid, tough, and without frills.

But you can't help noticing that the far right panel of black marble has already been erected, as if waiting for the engraver to arrive and fill in the details. A tribute, perhaps, to the man who, thanks to a severe heart attack, has had Australia's best-known near-death experience.

sacred sites

There are places in every city where history has happened. In many cases there is nothing to commemorate this fact. Even if there is a memorial, few seem to know about its existence. Yet these are the stepping stones to who and what we are. Let's visit some of the most important, and some not so serious, of these sites.

ANNANDALE AQUEDUCT

Sewer pipes do not usually appear on lists of significant sites, but the Annandale Aqueduct (to give it its more grandiose title) is an exception. There are two parts to this structure.

Gracefully supported by a series of elegant archways spanning a creek and three roadways (Nelson Street, Nelson Lane and Minogue Crescent), it first emerges from a sandstone cliff in a section of the Lew Hoad Reserve behind the Glebe–Leichhardt Police and Community Centre. It doesn't only look spectacular, this structure is also an engineering pioneer.

Built in 1895, the aqueduct was the first structure in Australia to use reinforced concrete. As ludicrous as it may sound these days, this created a major political controversy. The patent for this new method of construction was first taken out in 1874 by a French gardener, P. A .J. Monier, who used it, initially, to build stronger flower pots.

The idea of using this technique for a major engineering work was still largely experimental. In fact the Annandale project was bigger than any prior example of reinforced concrete construction in Europe.

Politics intervened. Before it was allowed to proceed, a Royal Commission investigated the aqueduct project and approval was given only on condition that the constructors, Carter Gummow and Co., personally guaranteed that it wouldn't fall down within three years.

It didn't. So far it's stayed up for a little more than a hundred and three years. In fact, the aqueduct easily pre-dates the elderly fig and palm tree that now overshadow it as it crosses over Hogan Park.

To celebrate its centenerary and then some, this stately old sewer pipe is currently being given a very well-deserved clean-up. As tempting as it is, crossing the bridge on foot is unfortunately not allowed. It would actually be quite a challenge, as it's only a metre wide and there is no safety fence. Still, no doubt many local kids have done so as a dare; the brave ones on bicycles.

The Annandale Aqueduct extends from the park at the intersection of Piper Street East and Trafalgar Lane in Annandale, to the Minogue Crescent section of the Lew Hoad Reserve in Glebe.

GILLIGAN'S ISLAND, TAYLOR SQUARE

The intersection in Darlinghurst known as Taylor Square is reputedly the most polluted part of Sydney, hardly surprising as four busy roads, including Oxford Street and the main road leading south from the Harbour Bridge, pass through here. The new Eastern Distributor may clear the air a little but don't stop holding your breath just yet.

It is also the gayest part of Sydney, being right in the constantly pumping heart of the city's pink triangle. Despite the constant flow of traffic, both automotive and human, there is still a small triangle of grass in the middle of Taylor Square that has become popularly known as Gilligan's Island. You may wonder why. I did. And while no official history has been recorded, word of mouth produced the following version of events.

For a decade or so this patch was the unofficial home of a small population of prolific drinkers who, oblivious to the pollution and the crowds, treated it as their personal island paradise. They would often sleep here after a hard day on the 'turps' and it was rare to drive past at any hour without seeing several in residence.

Sometime in the eighties, locals began to call this spot Gilligan's Island, after the television series. Certainly the inhabitants of this colony appeared to be as removed from the real world as any group of castaways.

Over the years the local council made several attempts to keep the natives happy. Palm trees were planted and sculptures were erected. Then one day the inhabitants of Gilligan's Island suddenly disappeared. Perhaps their ship finally came in.

An added touch of irony was provided by the fact that the nearest building to Gilligan's is Kinsela's, which is a very groovy night club set up in what was formerly a funeral parlour. Here the trendy young things in black could sip their designer drinks looking down on the islanders guzzling their budget booze. To me, the latter always looked like they were having more fun.

Gilligan's Island is at Taylor Square, approximately two kilometres east of the CBD, down Oxford Street.

GRAVE OF GRANNY SMITH

Next to the historic St Anne's church, lies the modest gravestone of Maria Ann Smith, deceased on March 9 1870 aged sixty-nine years.

Few would realise that this is a memorial to one of Australia's greatest women. As her epitaph suggests, 'so teach us to number our days that we may apply our hearts unto wisdom'.

It is only when you learn that Maria Smith is better known as Granny Smith that her claim to fame becomes apparent. It was she who discovered the Granny Smith apple and introduced it to the world.

Maria Smith came to Australia with her family from England in the early 1800s. Together with her husband she established a small orchard in what is now the suburb of Eastwood, just a few kilometres to the north of Ryde. In those days if you stood on the hill on which St Anne's is situated, most of what you would have seen would have been farmland, bush or, in the direction of Homebush Bay, mangrove swamp.

From the beginning, it was apparent that Maria Smith was a born leader. When it was taken to the markets for selling, all the farm produce bore the label 'Granny Smith'. Maria's husband obviously kept in the background.

According to one story, the Granny Smith apple was a freak of nature, a chance hybrid which developed on another tree. Still, Maria Smith was smart enough to realise the economic potential of this new variety and undertook what we would now call an extensive marketing campaign. At the produce markets, she asked for, and got, a premium price for her unique discovery.

She soon discovered that the demand for the Granny Smith apple—it is suitable for both eating and cooking, and stays fresher longer than other varieties—was greater than for any other. And its colour, a beautiful lime green, provided the perfect packaging.

Granny Smith's apple quickly took over her entire business. As other orchards decided they should grow these new apples, she found that she could sell seedlings grafted from the mother tree. The Australian apple which eventually bore her name was soon to become known throughout the world as the Granny Smith. And Maria Smith was possibly our first female entrepreneur. After her death in 1870, Granny Smith's orchard in Eastwood was eventually sold and subdivided. Nothing remains of it today. Tragically too, the original Granny Smith tree was chopped down and burnt for firewood, before horticulturalists were able to study how it had developed its unique fruit. At least there were enough seedlings to make sure the variety survived forever.

Granny Smith's gravestone, one of hundreds in this graveyard, may be the sole memorial to this remarkable woman, but she is in little danger of being forgotten. Her true legacy is still to be found in just about any fruit shop in Australia.

Granny Smith's grave is at St Anne's Church, on the busy intesection of Church Street and Victoria Road, Ryde.

TONY HANCOCK'S BUNGALOW, BELLEVUE HILL

F ans of the late British comedian Tony Hancock can make a pilgrimage to Bellevue Hill to witness the scene of Hancock's 'Last Half Hour'.

At one stage Hancock was the biggest drawcard in British showbiz, a star of television, radio and film. His *Hancock's Half Hour* series (first on radio, then on television) is now widely available on audiotape and video. It still ranks as one of the greatest comedy series ever produced.

But by the time Hancock came to Australia in 1968, he was a shell of his former self—alcoholic, depressed and, saddest of all, convinced he was no longer funny. Perhaps he wasn't. The audience booed him off the stage at a theatre in Brighton, Melbourne, when he turned up so drunk he was unable to stand upright. Later that year he arrrived in Sydney to appear in a series of local television specials that he hoped might jump-start his ailing career. He stayed here, in a small flat at the back of a friend's house.

For a while he stopped drinking and seemed to be back to normal. But when he started filming at the Channel Seven studios, it was obvious that he had lost his spark. The television specials were flops and were never shown. It was all too much for Tony.

On the night of June 25, he ended it all with a cocktail of vodka and pills. When he was found, he was still holding the butt of his final cigarette. A suicide note read, in part, 'Things seemed to go wrong too many times.' No. 181 is a private residence but if you look over the fence of the front car parking area at the block of flats next door, you will see Hancock's bungalow in the backyard to your left. Few people even realise that this is where he was staying at the time. Sadly, there is no indication that genius lived and died here.

Tony Hancock's bungalow is at No. 181 Birriga Road in Bellevue Hill. Please note this is a private residence.

HARRY'S CAFE DE WHEELS, WOOLLOOMOOLOO

It may be world famous, but today's Harry's Cafe is a world away from the original. What you are looking at now is a five-star silver-service restaurant compared to the first rustbucket establishment setup by Harry 'Tiger' Edwards in 1945 to provide some late night snacks for drunken sailors, prostitutes and taxi drivers.

While today's deluxe van may be a more suitable venue for celebrities like Pam Anderson and Elton John (two of many to have dined here), many miss the rough-as-guts charm of the original.

Call me old-fashioned, but this new one is like watching a technicolour remake of *On the Waterfront*. Photos show just how basic the old blue and yellow van used to be. With signs saying 'Harry's Snappy Snacks', 'Sargents Pies 'n' Peas' and 'Bert's Icy Cold Drinks' (no need for a menu, that was all there was) the only frills allowed were a couple of old Castrol oil drums for use as ashtrays and spitoons. Tables? Chairs? Who needs them?

The pies, however, were legendary, and a 1976 photo of Kentucky Fried Chicken founder Colonel Sanders chomping into one of Harry's finest is the highlight of his roadside portrait gallery.

Harry's Cafe de Wheels is on Cowper Wharf Roadway at Woolloomooloo, near the Finger Wharf.

GLEBE JOSS HOUSE AND 'WITCHES' HOUSES

After walking the gauntlet of Glebe Point Road's coffee shops and restaurants—congratulations if you made it through without spending any money—you may feel in need of some spiritual nourishment.

From Glebe Point Road turn left into Pendrill Street and walk downhill to Edwards Street. You will see the gates of a temple. It's called the 'Kwan Kung Temple' on the street sign, the 'Sze Yup Temple' on the gates, but to locals it's simply 'the Glebe Joss House'. This is one of the hidden delights of Sydney, an oasis of calm in the middle of the inner city. The gentle smell of incense hits you from a block away. While Australia's Chinese community are the main celebrants, respectful visitors of any faith are welcome.

If your spiritual tastes are more Catholic, it's only a short walk down Glebe Point Road to the Pope Paul VI Reserve on the edge of Blackwattle Bay. Here are two of the finest fig trees in Sydney, their canopies covering an area of a couple of suburban blocks. This is also a place for serenity—but not if you are in the water in a small fragile boat. It used to be thought that the harbour this far inland was too polluted for sharks. But it was here that a female rower was attacked by a shark, her craft nearly bitten in two.

If you stand near the water's edge and look west, you will notice three spires on the hill above the railway viaduct. These belong to a series of homes in Johnston Street, Annandale, that several generations of local kids have called 'the witches' houses'.

If you walk across Jubilee Park (a pleasure if you like palm trees, there are some of Sydney's oldest specimens planted here) and walk across to Johnston Street, you will clearly see why.

The Abbey, on the corner of Johnston and Weynton streets, is a rather remarkable gothic mansion with a definite Addams Family atmosphere, thanks to the ivy-covered walls and a needle spire adorned with gargoyles and a weather vane. It was built in 1881 by John Young, an eccentric local builder—but if kids want to believe that the place is haunted, so be it.

The Glebe Joss House is at the end of Pendrill Street, off Glebe Point Road. The 'Witches' houses are in Johnston Street, Annandale.

KOOKABURRA MEMORIAL, MOSMAN

I n a small park in the Sydney suburb of Mosman lies the memorial to one of Australia's forgotten aviation heroes. These days, few would recall the name of Keith Anderson, yet, in July 1929, his funeral procession was watched by more than six thousand mourners. They lined Bradleys Head Road in silence as his coffin, drawn by six horses, arrived at the Blessed Sacrament Church.

This was obviously a major event. Five Tiger Moth aircraft flew overhead in a cross formation, while eight RAAF planes skimmed the trees, dropping floral wreaths over the grave site. Who was this man?

Anderson, with his mechanic Bob Hitchcock, perished in the fierce desolation of the Tanami Desert, north-west of Alice Springs, while trying to locate the missing plane of Charles Kingsford Smith and Charles Ulm, the Southern Cross.

The pair set out from Sydney's Mascot airport in the *Kookaburra*, a tiny Westland Widgeon monoplane, despite a lack of navigational aids and a shortage of supplies. Forced to crash-land in the desert, hundreds of miles from civilisation, they soon died of thirst.

Kingsford Smith was eventually found near the Glenelg River by another search party and managed to fly his stricken plane to safety. Today we would consider Anderson's actions foolhardy, verging on suicidal. His plane was obviously unsuited to such a trip. But in the pioneering days of aviation, when flying really was as dangerous as it looked, Anderson's rescue attempt was seen as the height of heroism.

Ironically, a few months before, Anderson had tried to sue Kingsford Smith over a previous record-breaking flight. The lawsuit was unsuccessful, but as a peace offering, Kingsford Smith gave his former business partner a gift of money. It was with this money that Anderson had bought the ill-fated *Kookaburra*.

Perhaps this noble gesture inspired Anderson's desperate attempt to save a man he once considered a friend. Others, less kindly, suggested that the motive was publicity, a means to boost Anderson's public profile.

If so, he succeeded. The public breathlessly followed the saga in the daily papers and soon decided that Anderson was made of the right stuff. It was the public, not the government, who paid for the impressive memorial standing in Rawson Park, crowned with a Maltese Cross and elaborately carved with ivy designs. The inscription reads in part: 'The passing years shall leave him ageless, loved and unforgot'.

Not so. Smithy was the one to achieve immortality. His face features on Australian stamps and currency. He became a part of Australian folklore. After his burial, Anderson was very quickly 'forgot'.

He does however have one saving grace. Ironically for a man who died of thirst in the desert, in death he enjoys sweeping harbour views.

The Kookaburra *Memorial is in Rawson Park, next to the football oval, just off Bradleys Head Road.*

KURNELL CLIFF DWELLERS

As a relatively young nation, Australia can offer little in the way of significant archeological sites. But halfway up the cliffs at Kurnell, overlooking the spot where Captain Cook first entered Botany Bay, are the remains of what was once Sydney's most unique suburb.

It's uncertain when white settlers first decided to build shacks halfway up the cliff face at Kurnell, but during the Great Depression of the 1930s, with one in four Australians unemployed, shanty towns like these sprang up all along the coast.

Some shack communities still exist near Manly and at Stanwell Park, but the Kurnell shacks were the most architecturally spectacular, squeezed in the crevices of the sandstone walls, or suspended dramatically twenty metres over the water.

The residents always referred to their homes as 'weekend fishing cabins' (possibly to avoid the wrath of the taxman and the council), although some spent the majority of their lives here, rent free. Up until the 1970s, the local council turned a blind eye to this group but now, sadly, there is little sign of their existence, except for the remains of the occasional brick wall. They may have been squatters, but the Kurnell cliff dwellers had some of the best views in Sydney and, according to Elizabeth Cavanough's description in her 1967 book *Sydney Holiday*, all the mod cons of a city penthouse.

'A track led us down to the rocks and when we looked up we could see little houses tucked into the cliff ... then we met Mr. (Bert) Adamson who invited us to see over his home. His was a real cliff dwelling, like something you would never expect to see but only hear about. Above our heads as we entered the house was a large drum, draining fresh water through a home-made sand filter. The kitchen, living-room and bedroom were all cut out of the sandstone cliff and the whole place was comfortable and full of light. The blue ceiling and white walls reflected the colour of the sea, and there were plants growing in flower boxes along the windows.'

Most of the dwellings featured sinks and had fridges cooled by blocks of ice. Some had stoves and a chimney. As for food, there was a ladder leading to the rock platform for night fishing. It must have been an idyllic lifestyle, except for one unexpected danger. This was a popular spot for dumping stolen vehicles.

'Mr Adamson told us the last car to go over the cliff had taken his chimney and part of the roof with it,' writes Elizabeth Cavanough.

To visit this place is to be reminded of the Indian mesa communities in the Mojave Desert. Sadly, this unique slice of history is now gone, another victim of bureaucracy, and falling cars.

The former site of the Kurnell Cave Dwellers is in Captain Cook's Landing Place Reserve, Kurnell peninsula. It can be reached by rock-hopping around Sutherland Point from the Captain Cook Obelisk, or by taking the track down the cliffs, off Cape Solander Drive, near Inscription Point.

LAKE NORTHAM FOUNTAIN AND DAVE SANDS MEMORIAL

There are two tributes to sporting heroes near the intersection of Parramatta Road and Glebe Point Road. One is hard to miss, the other much less obvious. The yacht-shaped Lake Northam fountain in the middle of the lake in Victoria Park was erected in 1967 to celebrate the Gold Medal won at the 1964 Tokyo Olympics by yachtsman William Northam.

The fountain is a representation of the 5.5-metre-class yacht called *Barrenjoey*, which Northam sailed at the Games. Since being restored a few years ago, the fountain is now lit up at night.

There is a far less ostentatious sporting tribute directly opposite, at the base of the fountain in front of the curved Hall of Residence building at the end of Glebe Point Road. Here a modest marble plaque commemorates the death of part-Aboriginal boxer Dave Sands, one of six brothers who all fought in the ring. Dave won an Empire middleweight title.

He was only twenty-six when he died in 1952 in a car crash. Sands was much loved. 'A great Australian and gentleman and one of nature's greatest' reads the message on the plaque.

A typical Dave Sands story tells of the time his promoter threw a party after one of the fighter's many victories at Sydney Stadium. Dave didn't turn up and everyone wondered where the guest of honour had got to. He was found sitting on his suitcase at Central Station waiting to go home on the midnight mail train. When asked why he wasn't celebrating, he replied that he was. He had splashed out on two pies, one for now, and one for the journey. That was one more than his usual quota.

Some say that had he lived, Sands would have beaten anyone in his division, including superstars like Jake Lamotta and Sugar Ray Robinson.

In that case, you may be wondering why Northam's memorial is so much grander than Sands'. The answer probably lies in the fact that Northam, apart from being a top sportsman, was also a Sydney City alderman.

The Lake Northam fountain is in Victoria Park, adjacent to Parramatta Road. The Dave Sands memorial is at the intersection of Parramatta and Glebe Point roads. Both are in Glebe.

LANE COVE RIVER STEAK HOUSE AND THE SCENE OF THE BOGLE/CHANDLER MURDER MYSTERY

Who would guess that this patch of nature reserve, surrounded by well-to-do suburbia, has been the hotbed of so much crime and corruption? On the western bank of the Lane Cove River near Fullers Bridge, Chatswood, is a genuine slice of 1960s cuisine history, recalling an era when a charcoal grilled steak and a bottle of Dinner Ale was seen as the height of sophistication.

Nothing much has changed inside this white Spanish-style edifice. The toilet doors are still identified by those nostalgic silhouettes of a man in a top hat and a lady with a stylish perm. You can order a Fluffy Duck and a Harvey Wallbanger at the bar. A mural of a tropical island takes up one entire wall. And the steaks are still served up on a sizzling hot metal plate with the baked potato wrapped in foil.

With views of rowers training on the sluggish, brown river, it is a very pleasant place to have lunch or dinner, which perhaps explains why this was the favoured hang-out of Trevor Haken and his dodgy mates.

In 1995, after he rolled over and gave evidence at the NSW Royal Commission into Police Corruption, Haken openly confessed to being one of the State's most corrupt cops.

While stationed at Chatswood Police Station in the 1970s, Detective Haken was a regular visitor to the steak house, meeting three or four times a week with his mates to discuss such pressing matters as petty extortion and the fitting up of witnesses.

'They were the stingiest lot; they never tipped and they always wanted their red wine put on ice,' recalls Jayne.

She should know. She is the former waitress who met Haken while serving him bottles of chilled red, and later married him.

The current management, we should add, have nothing to do with whatever went on in the corner table two decades ago.

After dessert you may like to wander across Fullers Bridge and stroll along the bush track on the opposite bank of the river, in the direction of the Chatswood Golf Course. It may seem idyllic until you realise you have now entered perhaps the most famous crime scene in Australia's post-war history.

This is where the bodies of Dr Gilbert Bogle and Margaret Chandler were found early on New Year's Day, 1963. Both bodies, partly undressed, had been modestly covered with bits of cardboard or carpet. Articles of clothing had been neatly folded and placed on Bogle's body. There were no wounds and while there was evidence of vomiting, the post-mortem revealed no known poison.

But what turned this mystery into a national scandal was the fact that Bogle and Chandler were married—but not to each other. The couple had gone to the river, a popular lover's lane, after attending a wife-swapping party in nearby Chatswood.

Margaret Chandler had left the party with Bogle, a CSIRO scientist and Rhodes Scholar, after her own husband had left with another woman. Bogle had come alone, leaving his own wife at home with the four kids. The fact that these parties went on at all, let alone in a middle-class suburb like Chatswood, was to become the sensation of 1963.

The mystery has never been officially solved, which is why this case still haunts many people. Ken Nash, the host of the party, committed suicide exactly thirteen years after that fateful night.

The late Kit Denton, author and father of TV and radio star Andrew Denton, was also there. When I raised the subject with him nearly thirty years after the event, he refused to discuss the night at all. It must have been one hell of a party.

The Lane Cove River Steak House is on the western bank of the Lane Cove River, near Fullers Bridge, Chatswood.

MARY McKILLOP MUSEUM, NORTH SYDNEY

Here's a rare example of the sacred meeting the satirical. When it was decided to start a museum devoted to Australia's first saint, Mary McKillop, the Sisters of Saint Joseph hired a creative director, Tony Sattler, best remembered for wicked social satire.

Tony was the co-creator of *The Naked Vicar Show*, a 1970s television series which featured, as its logo, a nude man wearing a clerical collar. Sattler also wrote and produced sitcoms like *Kingswood Country*. If he seemed an unlikely choice to set up a religious museum, the Mary McKillop experience is all the more enjoyable for it. This is a fun interactive voyage through a saint's life.

A potential problem for the museum founders was obvious. As a nun who had taken vows of poverty, she left few possessions. There's a veil, rosary beads, a couple of hankies—not enough to fill a suitcase, let alone a museum. The museum gets around this with a variety of multimedia tricks, including a re-enactment of Mary's excommunication featuring an animatronic bishop.

Among several interactive displays is one showing the mean streets in which Mary's Sisters of Saint Joseph worked. You can choose any of six voice buttons: amputee, street kid, prostitute, drunk, single mother and thief. The prostitute button is the most popular.

There is another touch of controversy. What was once claimed as Australia's biggest Aboriginal artwork, a representation by Sakshi Anmatyerre, is painted on the ceiling. Unfortunately, it was later found that the artist is not aboriginal but was born in India. At the time of writing, the Sisters of Saint Joseph were deciding what to do with their fake artwork.

Like any good museum, Mary McKillop Place has a souvenir shop, which is full of McKillop merchandise. You can buy Mary McKillop fridge magnets and souvenir spoons but, on my last visit, they had yet to produce Saint Mary snow domes. Hopefully this oversight will be remedied soon.

Mary McKillop Place is at 7 Mount Street, North Sydney. For further details, phone 02 9954 9900.

MO'S HOUSE, KENSINGTON

Roy Rene, better known to millions of Australians as Mo, was Australia's best loved comedian throughout the 1930s and 1940s. He helped Australia laugh its way through the Great Depression, at a time when one in four Australians were out of work.

When Jack Benny saw him perform during World War II, he commented, 'I can't understand a word of what this guy's talking about, but he's one of the funniest men I've ever seen.'

Mo would have been the first to agree with Benny's assessment. At one stage, Mo was so well-known that a letter sent from New Zealand, with only a caricature of Mo on the front, was delivered immediately to his home.

It would have been delivered to this house, in Cottenham Avenue, where Roy Rene lived most of his life with his wife and two kids. It is strange that while other icons of that era like Don Bradman and Phar Lap have been fittingly honoured (Phar Lap three times—his heart in Canberra, his body in Melbourne and his headstone at Sydney's Royal Randwick racecourse) the only tribute to Mo is a theatrical awards presentation posthumously named after him. Mo would have been spitting at some of the acts that win one of his statuettes.

None of the current residents of Cottenham Avenue appear to know that genius once resided at No. 29. This is no celebrity mansion with a huge security fence. It is an ordinary house in an ordinary street, chosen, I suspect, because of its closeness to Randwick Racecourse (Roy was an enthusiastic if mug punter).

The only difference between this house and any other is the sign on the front wall reading, 'bore water in use'. Sounds like one of Mo's punchlines.

Born of Dutch Jewish parents in Adelaide, Roy Rene's genius was not in what he said, but in what he didn't say. He had the rare ability to make you think what he was thinking, especially when he was thinking unspeakable thoughts.

My fondest memory of Roy Rene is captured in Fred Parson's biography, describing how Roy, in his latter years of failing health, would drive down to Coogee Beach 'for a breath of fresh air'. He would sit in his Buick, reading the form guide with the windows wound up tight, the inside of the car filling up with acrid cigar smoke.

Roy Rene retired in 1953 and died in November 1954. If you're ever in the neighbourhood, walk past Mo's house and think unspeakable thoughts in his honour.

Mo's house is at No. 29 Cottenham Avenue, Kensington. Please note that this is a private residence.

MR ETERNITY, SYDNEY SQUARE

For more than thirty years, Arthur Stace roamed the dawn streets of Sydney writing one word, 'Eternity', on the footpath in yellow chalk or crayon. He began his life's mission in 1930, after attending a sermon by the Reverend John Ridley at the Burton Street Baptist Church in Darlinghurst. The closing words were, 'Where will you spend Eternity?'

From that moment, Stace gave up his life of petty crime and hard drinking and devoted the rest of his life to seeking, and writing, 'Eternity'.

Stace died in 1967 having written, by his estimate, the word at least 500,000 times. Fifty times a day was his minimum workload. He didn't seek publicity, preferring to work anonymously in the early hours before dawn, so it wasn't until late in his career that he was finally identified, interviewed and photographed.

'The funny thing is that before I wrote it (Eternity) I could hardly write my own name,' he explained. 'I couldn't have spelt Eternity for a hundred quid, but it came out smoothly and in a beautiful copperplate script. I couldn't understand it and I still can't.'

Stace claimed that, for him, writing 'Eternity' was as much a miracle as talking in tongues. No wonder the legend of Arthur Stace, better known as Mr Eternity, remains one of Sydney's best-loved parables.

Clive James has written a poem about Stace—that 'scuttling ratbag' as he affectionately describes him. Sydney artist Martin Sharp has incorporated the magic word into several of his paintings. And the message lives on forever in Sydney Square, near the corner of George Street and Bathurst Street, close to Town Hall station. Here, at the base of the fountain in front of St Andrews Cathedral, is the familiar one-word sermon, set permanently in a paving stone. By coincidence, or maybe by fate, the architect of the Sydney Square redevelopment which included this tribute in 1977 was a relative of the preacher who first inspired Stace to embark on his mission.

Part of the charm of Stace's chosen method was the obvious impermanence of writing in chalk or crayon. The eternal word would disappear in the next shower or rainstorm. But one Eternity, miraculously, remains.

One day Arthur Stace managed to climb the tower of the GPO building (corner George Street and Martin Place) and write on the metal surface of the bell. His final Eternity was still there when a documentary was made about his life a few years ago, and hopefully will remain so for an eternity to come.

The Mr Eternity tribute is in Sydney Square (subject to current renovations), near the corner of George and Bathurst streets. It may be nearly impossible to get up there to see it, but it's good to know it's there.

'No. 96' Block of Flats

I t may be more than twenty-five years since it first exploded onto our TV screens, but the adults-only soapie 'No. 96' (1972 to 1977) is in little danger of ever being forgotten.

At the time it was billed as the soap that ended Australian TV's innocence, and for once the hype was accurate. 'No. 96' featured nudity, nymphomania, thrill killings, homosexuality and transsexuality (often in the same episode) and the shock/horror storylines would be seen as raunchy even today.

It was so sensational that the only way to end the series was to blow up the entire cast.

Based around a supposedly typical block of suburban flats, most of the series was filmed at the Channel Ten Studios, but the apartment block at No. 83 Moncur Street Woollahra (with a styrofoam 'No. 96' stuck above the front door) was used for the opening and closing credits. The stairs and numbered doors of the flats, which look pretty much as they did in the series, were frequently used for identifying scenes.

This was enough to convince most people that the action really did happen here. At one stage the place was so notorious that every self-respecting bus tour of Sydney would include a trip down Moncur Street, while passengers kept an eye out for Abigail in a see-thru negligee, being stalked by the pantihose strangler.

The owners of what is officially called Moncur Flats (opened in 1929 according to a plaque on the wall) have since disguised the building by painting it pale green. But this doesn't fool devoted 'No. 96' fans, who still hum the catchy theme song whenever they drive past.

There are eight flats in the building and, in the interests of cultural heritage, I can reveal exclusively where some of the original cast lived during their fictional tenancy (where they slept was another matter).

Flat 1 (bottom left) was originally the Continental Deli run by Aldo Godolfus (Johnny Lockwood) and his wife Roma (Philippa Baker).

Above them, in Flat 4, lived homosexual lawyer Don Finlayson, played by Joe Hasham, whose occasional flatmate and bedmate was Bev Houghton, the character turned into a national sex symbol by Abigail.

Vera Collins (the sophisticated fashion designer played by Elaine Lee) lived in Flat 8, top left.

Resident dag Arnold Feather (Jeff Kevin) shared the top right flat with Alf and Lucy Sutcliffe. Lucy's additional claim to fame was that she was played by actress Elisabeth Kirkby, later to become a well-respected MP in real life.

The much-loved Dorrie and Herb (Pat McDonald and Ron Shand) lived in Flat 3 above Norma's Wine Bar.

Sadly, both the deli and the wine bar have now been superceded by more mundane businesses, namely a doctor's surgery and an art dealer's gallery.

Considering what supposedly went on here during the reign of 'No. 96' (Aldo's deli was fire-bombed for starters, and satanic rituals went on inside) the place appears to have survived very well. I'm reliably informed that the current tenants behave very respectably indeed.

The No. 96 *flats are at 83 Moncur Street, Woollahra. These are now private residences.*

SHARPIE'S GOLF HOUSE NEON

For the last fifty odd years, a neon golfer has been putting a neon ball into a neon hole (he's good this guy, he never misses) on top of a building in Elizabeth Street.

Exact details of the most famous neon sign in Sydney are scant, but the current owners of what is now known as Sharpie's Golf House suggest the sign dates back to at least 1952, when Jack Landis ran a shop called the Golf House on the site. The word 'Sharpie's' is a fairly recent (1985) but sympathetic addition to the sign.

In fact, the sign is owned by Claude Neon, who originally designed and constructed it. Lindsay Sharp, a former golf pro and the current owner of Sharpie's, foots the electricity bill (which must be considerable—the sign is on from dusk to 4am seven days a week).

He does this with good grace, and is the first to realise how important a part of the public face of the city his sign has become. It has been featured on promotional videos along with internationally recognised icons such as the Opera House and the Harbour Bridge.

Another indication of the sign's popularity is how quickly the owners are told if, as happens occasionally, part of the sign malfunctions.

'Hey mate, the bloke's lost his ball' is the most common complaint.

There is a level of affection for this sign that has no parallel with modern works of neon. When the sign had to be switched off for three months due to renovations, people phoned up afterwards to say how much they had missed the little guy. To many travellers arriving in Sydney at night from nearby Central Station, the Sharpie's sign represents an official welcome to the city.

As befits its status as Sydney's best-loved neon, the Sharpie's sign is heritage-listed. Hopefully the little neon golfer will be putting away for another fifty years.

Sharpie's Golf House is at 220 Elizabeth Street in the city.

STAR OF THE EAST AMPHITHEATRE

Believe it or not, there was once a white temple on the northern end of Balmoral Beach, strategically placed so that members of a bizarre religious cult could witness the Second Coming of Christ.

According to the members of the Order of the Star of the East, He would arrive in the form of Indian guru Krishnamurti, walking across the waters of Sydney Harbour.

The amphitheatre, based on the architectural style of Grecian temples, rates as possibly the most extraordinary building in Sydney's history. Until you see the photographic evidence, it's hard to believe it was actually there.

The Star Amphitheatre, as it was most commonly known, was built in the 1920s at a cost of more than 15,000 pounds. Most of this money was raised via donations from the more gullible members of Sydney society. For a fee of between ten and a hundred pounds, donors could book a seat in the amphitheatre which would give them, according to the sales pitch, a panoramic view of Christ's promised arrival through the Heads. The donor's name was engraved on each seat as a semi-permanent reservation. The seats were theirs for the next twenty-five years.

The Second Coming project (some would call it a scam) emanated from another extraordinary building, The Manor, which still stands on the corner of Iluka Road and Morella Road in nearby Clifton Gardens.

This fifty-room mansion, also known as Bakewell's Folly, was built by the Sydney trader Thomas Bakewell before being taken over by the Theosophical Society. Various members of this society, notably Bishop Leadbeater and Annie Besant, set up the Star of the East sect in 1922. They started negotiations with Krishnamurti and began buying prime waterfront real estate at Edwards Beach, the small cove immediately north of Balmoral Beach.

In 1926, The Manor also became the first headquarters of a new radio station. It was called 2GB after the initials of the Theosophist patron saint Giordano Bruno. Naturally, 2GB was granted the world rights to the 'live and exclusive' coverage of the Second Coming, if and when it happened.

These days, 2GB is a slightly more commercial radio station, but if this major event does ever happen, they have a couple of rugby league commentators on staff who could give a running commentary.

It was the aforementioned Bishop Leadbeater, a clairvoyant and medium as well as spiritual real estate salesman, who first floated the theory that Christ, in the guise of Krishnamurti, would return at a day and time to be announced. This revelation was enough to get the donations flowing in.

Once built, the blue and white amphitheatre was a wondrous sight to behold. Three storeys high, with spectacular views of the beach and the harbour, it had seating for 3,000 paying customers, a library, a meditation room and, on the ground floor, a popular tea room.

Lectures—'admission free, collection'—were held to explain how and why Christ would choose Balmoral as his born-again Jerusalem. How and why, but not when. The actual date of arrival was never mentioned.

Sadly, Christ never did make it to Balmoral. Nor did Krishnamurti, who pulled out of the project after disagreements with Leadbeater. Factional fighting among the various leaders of the cult eventually caused its sudden demise in 1929. Those who had made reservations, realising they had been duped, quickly removed their brass plaques from their seats with screwdrivers.

The amphitheatre was eventually sold in the 1930s and used for open-air vaudeville shows. Apparently summer evening performances under full moonlight were spectacular occasions, although less so when it rained.

With its paint peeling and its concrete crumbling, the Star Amphitheatre was last used as the world's strangest mini golf centre. It was pulled down in the 1950s and has since been replaced by a nondescript brown block of flats. To my knowledge, there is no evidence, apart from photos, that it ever existed. Perhaps that's the way Christ would have wanted it.

The amphitheatre used to stand on the corner of Edwards Bay Road and Wyargine Street, overlooking Edwards Beach.

SYDNEY STADIUM

I t was cold and draughty, the acoustics were terrible and when it rained, you couldn't hear anything. But the old Sydney Stadium at Rushcutters Bay had something no architect can design—atmosphere, oodles of it.

It also had a nickname. They called it the 'The Old Barn' or 'The Tin Shed', mainly because it had more of the feel of an ageing warehouse than an entertainment complex. Yet all the greats, from Sinatra to the Beatles, from Count Basie to Sarah Vaughan, played here until the place was ripped down in the early 1970s to make way for, of all things, a viaduct for the new railway line to Bondi Junction.

The new Entertainment Centre which eventually replaced the shed as Sydney's premier entertainment venue may have heating, comfy seats and clean toilets, but will people ever talk about it in the same way as people talk about the Stadium? I doubt it.

Today there is a small plaque on the triangle of land at the corner of New South Head Road and Neild Avenue, opposite Rushcutters Bay Park. It's there, trust me, but you probably can't see it because it's been surrounded by a people-proof cyclone fence. This is the only memorial to the place where thousands of show business and sporting legends once performed.

The Tin Shed was especially famous as a boxing and wrestling venue. In the 1950s and 1960s, boxing at the Stadium was a weekly ritual. The late Sir Frank Packer managed a troupe of boxers, as did rival newspaper proprietor Ezra Norton, along with numbers of colourful gentlemen with shady backgrounds, like illegal casino owner Perc Galea. This was part of the unique atmosphere. Here crims mingled freely with millionaires. It was the kind of joint Damon Runyon used to write about.

World Championship Wrestling—two parts theatre, one part sport—also took place here. Skull Murphy, King Curtis, Mario Milano—they are all part of this place.

But the Stadium tradition goes back much further than that. The most famous event in its history was the 1908 World Heavyweight title. Here the reigning champion, Tommy Burns from Canada, met the formidable challenger, Jack Johnson, the giant negro from Texas.

Billed as the fight of the century, for once reality managed to live up to the hype. Not only was this the first heavyweight title to be held in Australia, it was also the first time a black man had been allowed to compete for the ultimate world boxing crown.

Jack Johnson, who looked like a cross between Mike Tyson and Michael Jordan, proved to be the crowd favourite. He was brash and flamboyant, and like a man called Ali more than five decades later, liked to taunt his rivals in the ring. He was heavily backed to win.

The promoter of the fight, newspaper proprietor Hugh D. McIntosh, was also the man who, a year earlier, first decided to build a stadium on this site. Before then this land had been a Chinese market garden.

This first Sydney Stadium had no roof and the then incredible capacity of 20,000 people. On the morning of Boxing Day 1908, McIntosh must have wished he had built it three times the size. The stadium was quickly filled to the brim, and so was Rushcutters Bay Park, with all those supporters who couldn't get in.

This was the sporting event which really set Australia on the map, attracting reporters from around the world, including the novelist Jack London. The fight itself was a bloodbath, with the police rushing into the ring in the fourteenth round to stop proceedings before Burns was seriously injured. Johnson, without a scratch on his smiling face, was declared the new World Champion, starting a fine tradition of black heavyweight champions. Burns, valiant in defeat, had been beaten to a pulp.

In 1912, with the proceeds from this historic fight, McIntosh put a roof on the stadium and next year sold it to the legendary Reg 'Snowy' Baker. Under his reign, it was known briefly as 'Baker's Stadium'. He was a remarkably versatile sportsman (competing at high levels in twenty-nine different sports) who also acted as referee at Sydney Stadium boxing tournaments. He was also an actor and stuntman in Australian movies, once performing an eighty-foot dive into Sydney Harbour. He later went to Hollywood to live, where, among other feats, he taught Rudolf Valentino how to perform horse-riding tricks and Douglas Fairbanks Snr how to crack a whip.

When asked to describe his greatest sporting moments, Baker referred to a match at the Sydney Stadium between an American, Eddie McGoorty, and an Australian Aboriginal, Jerry Jerome. Baker was referee, but on this occasion he managed to get too closely involved in the match. McGoorty threw a wild punch that landed squarely on Baker's chin. The refferree hit the ropes and fell on his back. McGoorty picked up Baker, shook hands with him as if to apologise, then continued with the fight.

The star from this period was a handsome young middleweight from East Maitland, Les Darcy. For a brief time, Darcy captured the public imagination like no other boxer. He is usually grouped with Don Bradman, Walter Lindrum and Phar Lap as the true sporting heroes of this century. The Stadium was his place.

Sydney Stadium was certainly no architectural masterpiece. Despite its age, it somehow always looked as if it was just a temporary wall covered with billboards. But what it did have, apart from atmosphere, was two memorable neon signs above its Gate 2 entrance on the corner.

To the left, above the word 'BOXING', two battered pugs squared up. To the right, above the word 'WRESTLING', two brawlers engaged in head-locks. Between them, a neon kangaroo stood below the word 'STADIUM'. To many old-timers this was the gateway to paradise.

While researching this book, I asked a veteran sports reporter what happened to these old signs. I was amazed to hear that they were simply thrown out on the tip, as were most of the old photos and posters that lined the walls and the offices. What a tragedy.

Another sacred site lies just across the road but it too has, literally, bitten the dust. Up until 1996, the Rushcutter Travelodge stood on the north side of New South Head Road next to Rushcutters Bay Park, along with the tenpin bowling centre where John Lennon rolled down some balls during the Beatles' Australian tour in 1964.

But the Travelodge's main claim to fame, as any self-respecting Sydney cabbie used to tell you every time they drove past, was as the place where Billy Snedden died—'on the job'.

Sir Billy Snedden, a former Federal Cabinet Minister, Liberal Party leader and Speaker of the House of Representatives, had a heart attack in his hotel room on June 27 1987. He was aged sixty. The big question was, who was he with at the time?

Melbourne's notorious *Truth* newspaper, acting on information allegedly supplied by a senior Darlinghurst police officer, gleefully reported that Snedden 'died happy', was still wearing a condom when found, and 'it was loaded'.

Rumours spread like wildfire throughout Sydney's bistros and hair salons. Most centred on one woman, a prominent fashion designer. This woman, Prue Acton, went to extraordinary lengths to prove it couldn't have been her, eventually issuing a statement to the media. It had been prepared by her lawyer and was complete with airline flight details showing that she was in Tasmania at the time.

It wasn't her, but in Sydney the facts rarely get in the way of a good rumour, and to this day you will still hear the one about Billy and Prue down at Rushcutter Travelodge.

The motel is no more, replaced by a swish new apartment block, but will that destroy the myth? I doubt it.

The Sydney Stadium is on the corner of New South Head Road and Neild Avenue, Rushcutters Bay.

WHITLAMS' HOUSE, CABRAMATTA

To most baby boomers, the 1972 Federal Election on the hot summer's night of December 2 was a defining moment, perhaps the only election where people can still pinpoint what they were doing on the night.

The Australian Labor Party, headed by Gough Whitlam, represented the hopes of many people for social change. They appealed to the young adult vote by staging Australia's first pop campaign, complete with a jingle sung by celebrities like Little Pattie. The slogan, 'It's Time', accurately summed up the mood of the era.

Many people threw parties to watch the election results on television, a new phenomenon that inspired David Williamson's play *Don's Party*, later to be made into a film.

But where did Gough Whitlam have his own celebration party? Right here, at No. 32 Albert Street, in the outer western suburb of Cabramatta.

This was where the Whitlams had been living since 1957, in the heart of the working-class Werriwa electorate. The only difference between this house and all the others in Albert Street is the flat roof, which makes it look more like a beach shack than a family home. It somehow looks much too small to house a family noted for their great height.

It's hard to believe that this humble abode, which looks as if it hasn't been painted since the election, was the scene of one of the greatest political events this century.

At 11.27pm, seated on a white piano stool in the backyard, Gough Whitlam made a nationwide announcement. 'All I want to say at this stage is that it is clear that the majority given by NSW, Victoria and Tasmania is so substantial that the Government will have a very good mandate to carry out all its policies,' he began.

He couldn't say much more because, forty kilometres away, in the much more upmarket suburb of Bellevue Hill, Prime Minister William MacMahon had yet to officially concede defeat.

It was a Whitlam family tradition to spend election night at home and Gough resisted pressure from Labor Party advisers to move to a larger venue.

'The crowd, they warned, would be too big for the small cottage and its pocket-handkerchief garden,' wrote Laurie Oakes and David Solomon in their book on the campaign. 'Whitlam insisted that the function would be held at the house as usual. The party workers in the electorate expected it, he said, and that was that.'

The main concession to the importance of the occasion was to hire a couple of Portaloos and stick a satellite dish on the roof.

It was a very hot night and with an estimated 500 people shoehorned into the house and the backyard, tempers were strained. Fights broke out between television and radio reporters, all trying to capture the historic moment.

Gough Whitlam spent the early part of that evening in Room 7, the main executive suite at the Sunnybrook Motel, two blocks away at 355 Hume Highway. Here, four television sets and seven telephones were placed around a room so that Whitlam and his closest advisors could evaluate

14. Alfred Hitchcock experiences vertigo at The Gap during his 1960 visit.

15. A bird's eye view of the inner-city wetlands created by businessman Max Frost.

16. A personal tribute to Albert Namatjira in Bondi.

17. *The car (no longer) up the tree.*

JOHNSON v BURNS

18. *Jack Johnson knocks down Tommy Burns in Sydney Stadium in 1908, winning the World Heavyweight title, as depicted on a cigarette card of the period.*

19. The scene of the crime. At this spot the bodies of Gilbert Bogle and Margaret Chandler were found on New Year's Day, 1963.

20. The fabulous Sydney Stadium, where Frank Sinatra once performed. All that remains today is a small, hidden memorial.

21. The mysterious crashing plane of Minchinbury.

22. *John Cann, the snake charmer of La Perouse.*

23. *Auburn Gardens, a little bit of Japan hidden in the western suburbs of Sydney.*

24. It looks like Kyoto but it's actually in Auburn Gardens.

25. June 1964, and Beatlemania erupts in front of the Sheraton Wentworth Hotel in Potts Point.

26. One of the thousands of antiquities collected by Professor Charles Nicholson, on display at his private museum within the University of Sydney.

the results in privacy. When it became clear that he had won, he returned home to announce the victory.

The current manager of the motel can still remember the excitement of that night but sadly Whitlam's executive suite has long been demolished and replaced by a new building complex.

One can only imagine how Gough Whitlam must have felt as he was driven the short distance home from the motel through the quiet suburban streets of Cabramatta, suddenly aware that he now had the most important job in the country.

The Whitlams no longer live here, and few Australians would even be aware that history happened in this most ordinary of streets. Cabramatta is now one of the main centres of settlement for Australia's recent influx of Vietnamese migrants, many of whom, I suspect, would be unaware of who Gough Whitlam is, let alone that he once lived in the same suburb.

There is one other place of interest to those who are in the neighbour-hood. Just down the road, at the intersection of Governor Macquarie Drive and the Hume Highway, is Sydney's other Harbour Bridge. This replica may be several sizes smaller than the one joining Dawes Point to Milsons Point, but it has one major point of difference. You can drive underneath it. The bridge marks the entrance to a huge complex of new and used car yards. It was officially opened in 1988 by NSW Police Minister George Paciullo. Have your photo taken standing underneath and amaze your friends.

The Whitlam's House is at 32 Albert Street, Cabramatta. Please note that this is a private residence.

YABBA AT THE SCG SPORTSPACE! TOUR

Up until his death in 1942, Stephen Gascoigne was almost as well-known in cricketing circles as Don Bradman. Better known as Yabba, Gascoigne was Australia's best-known spectator, renowned for his booming foghorn of a voice. On a clear day, Yabba could be heard from all parts of the Sydney Cricket Ground.

Yabba was famous for his deep knowledge of the game and his quick wit. 'Your length is lousy but you bowl a good width' is a Yabba original. He also introduced comments like 'get a bag' and 'ava go you mug' which have now become part of the Austalian vernacular.

So it is only fitting that on the Sportspace! tour of the famous Sydney Cricket Ground, Yabba should be celebrated. This is done in a unique way by hiring an actor to portray him.

Jack Mayers, big and beefy like the man himself, was hired after an unusual audition that involved standing at the other end of the ground and screaming his lungs out. Mayers' research into his character involved long hard hours spent in pubs watching how the average Australian bloke walks and talks. He wears the same style of hat and carries the kind of Gladstone bag in which Yabba used to bring his lunch and two (never more) bottles of beer.

Yabba always sat on the Hill, a piece of sacred turf at the southern end of the ground. Now replaced with a modern grandstand, this area is commemorated with a sign saying Yabba's Hill. He will never be forgotten, which is more than you can say for some of the criceters he watched.

Sportspace! tours are held on non-match days at 10am, 1pm and 3pm. Yabba is not included in abbreviated tours of less than twenty people. Phone 02 9380 0383 for details. The Sydney Cricket Ground is off Moore Park Road, Moore Park.

hidden

treasures

One of the joys of any city is to stumble
upon the totally unexpected. These are the
special places worth pointing out to friends
as you pass. Most deserve a detour. Some
are worth a visit. Even if you never get to
see them, it's wonderful to know that they
are there.

ALBERT STATUE, BONDI

There is a statue of Albert (Queen Victoria's husband) in front of the Hyde Park Barracks in Macquarie Street in the city. But there is a much more moving statue of Albert (Namatjira, the Aboriginal artist) in the heart of Bondi. Each weekend, tens of thousands drive past it when they turn right off Old South Head Road into O'Brien Street. Most are oblivious to the fact that a unique work of art is hiding just metres from the traffic lights.

In a tiny front courtyard this larger-than-life size statue of Australia's own Albert sits under a bush. It was sculpted about five years ago by a professional stone carver who lives in the flat upstairs.

The work was created for a sculpture project that failed to eventuate, so 'Albert', as the work is called, has remained here patiently watching the world pass by. This, in fact, is where he was created. The original hunk of sandstone was too big to move upstairs or down the back so, during the creative process, locals driving past were able to see Albert evolving on a week-by-week basis.

Although Albert is apparently for sale, most locals agree it would be a shame to see him move. Bondi is his spiritual home.

If you want to have a closer look at Albert, cross Old South Head Road at the O'Brien Street lights and walk up the hill to No. 230 (on the north side of the road, furthest from the beach). The artist has requested people not to enter his property, but the statue can be easily enjoyed from the footpath.

The Albert Statue is at 230 Old South Head Road, Bondi.

BOB ASKIN'S HOUSE, FAIRY BOWER BEACH, MANLY

Sir Robert Askin, 'Bobbie' to his mates, is best remembered for those four magic words, 'ride over the bastards'. He is alleged to have said this when, as premier of New South Wales, he was seated in the back of a limo with visiting US President Lyndon Johnson and Australian prime minister Harold 'all the way with LBJ' Holt.

This was 1966, at the height of the Vietnam War, and protestors were lying on the road in Liverpool Street in front of the car. Askin later said 'ride over the bastards' wasn't exactly what he had said, but joked that the comment did him a lot of good.

Bob Askin was the son of a tram driver from Glebe who went on to become one of the longest-serving premiers of NSW. He resigned in 1975 after close to ten continuous years in power. The Askin period was remarkable for a dramatic rise in organised crime and constant allegations of police corruption.

During the Askin years, illegal casinos operated more or less openly. Every taxi driver in Sydney would happily drop you off at the 33 Club or the Forbes Club without you having to give directions. At these clubs, your fellow gamblers around the baccarat tables would probably include top cops and senior members of the legal fraternity.

Rumours that Askin might be profiting from the proceeds of illegal gambling gained impetus when, in 1971, he sold the cosy bungalow he and his wife Mollie had lived in since the war. They moved up to a new split-level house at No. 86 Bower Street in Fairy Bower, next to the southern end of Manly Beach. Here they lived for the rest of their lives.

This impressive new house had splendid water views, a swimming pool and a specially designed dirt garden for Ginger and Kitty, the Askins' two beloved stray cats. The Askins had no children.

Askin claimed to be a man of simple pleasures. His idea of a good time was to drop into the Manly Hotel for a beer with his RSL mates, to go to the races occasionally, or to stroll along the beach eating an ice-cream. But this man-of-the-people image was shattered somewhat when Askin died of a heart attack in 1981. He left an estate worth close to $2 million, most of it going to Mollie and members of his staff.

By the time Mollie Askin died in March 1984, her personal estate, including Bobbie's millions, had dramatically escalated to more than $3.7 million. Before probate was granted, curious examiners from the Taxation Department tried to work out where the Askin fortune had come from. According to his own records, a considerable percentage was attributed to 'race winnings'.

Since then, 'I won it at the races' has become a popular Sydney euphemism. And since then, the Askin multimillion-dollar mansion has become a Sydney icon, worth checking out next time you stroll along Manly Beach eating an ice-cream.

For the best views, take Marine Parade, the pathway next to the sand past Manly Surf Club. The former Askin house is the big white one just past Bower Lane. Look for the glass-fronted balcony. Bobbie, Mollie, Ginger and Kitty lived here.

Bob Askin's house is at 86 Bower Street, Fairy Bower Beach, Manly. Please note this is a private residence.

AUBURN JAPANESE GARDENS

T he suburb of Auburn in Sydney's west is a prime example of multi-culturalism at work. Over the last twenty years, this area has become a suburban mecca for the Muslim community. It may say something about contemporary Australian society that the most dominant symbols of this region are the golden arches of Silverwater McDonald's and the rocket-like spires of the new mosque on North Parade. The mosque has the bigger impact—those spires can be seen for kilometres. But there is also a little slice of Kyoto in Auburn.

The Japanese Gardens were first opened in 1977 but the trees have already achieved a surprising degree of maturity. A more recent feature of the gardens is the mini-mountain, still a work-in-progress but rapidly taking shape. Like a stage backdrop, this mountain is designed to be seen from a distance, but even up close it's much bigger than a molehill.

The large central lake is already well-populated with a wide variety of ducks, while a pair of aggro white swans have moved in and taken over. There's no question who's the boss of this pond. There's a sign warning children to keep out of their way.

Around the lake are typically Japanese additions like a tea pavilion and a set of stepping stones that should test anyone's sense of balance. If you do fall in, you will be able to check out some of the lake's very large koi carp. Another sign indicates that there is a $500 fine for carp theft, not surprising when you consider that prime examples of these fish can fetch a small fortune.

There are many avid breeders of these ornamental fish in Sydney (Harry M. Miller among them) and the finest stud carp are bought and sold at auction just like more traditional forms of livestock. Carp auctions are sometimes held in these gardens, well worth a visit even if you only want to watch. Don't scratch your ear; you could end up with a $1,000 goldfish.

The most recent addition to the Japanese Gardens is a replica of the famous rock and gravel zen garden at the Ryoanji Temple in Kyoto. It may take another millenium for Auburn's rocks to achieve the spiritual power of those in Kyoto, or maybe not.

The gardeners have resorted to high technology to speed up the process. A system of plastic drippers is in place to encourage the speedy formation of moss and lichen on the rocks.

At Ryoanji the surface is raked daily according to a sacred pattern, but when I last looked at Auburn, the gravel was unmarked except for a sign in the middle saying, 'please keep off'. There may be a job vacancy going here for someone with a diploma in zen rakecraft.

Also within the Auburn complex is a small wildlife reserve, featuring native animals including koalas, wallabies and kangaroos. There's also an an impressive aviary. Barbecue facilities make this an ideal picnic location.

But for me the real treasure is the Bonsai Garden, mainly because it is such a secret surprise. It took me three visits before I stumbled upon it. The entrance gate is the other side of the toilets, through the kiosk area, past a shop selling tacky souvenirs. But once inside the gates you could be in another country and another century. This magic space, designed by local bonsai enthusiasts Ron Flack and Elizabeth Simeonoff, was opened in 1988 but the feeling here is timeless. High walls screen out the outside world and gravel paths with stepping stones add to the charm. You could easily imagine you were in the courtyard of an imperial palace, circa 1399 AD.

That year springs to mind because one of the feature exhibits is the recreation of a bonsai depicted on a Japanese scroll dating from the fourteenth century.

Most of the trees featured here are very old, donated by either clubs or generous individuals. Some are large by bonsai standards, like the group planting of spruce in a cement tray container that must have arrived on the back of a truck.

Time appears to stop in here. It's a wonderful place to sit and think. Equally interesting is the reaction of other people as they walk through the gates. Everyone begins to whisper, as if they have entered a cathedral. This is a sacred place.

Auburn Japanese Gardens are part of the Auburn Botanic Gardens. The entrance is in Chisholm Road, opposite the intersection of Chiswick Road. The Bonsai Garden is open 10am to 3pm (Monday to Friday) and 10am to 4pm (Saturdays and Sundays). There is no admission fee.

BEST VIEW IN SYDNEY: DOVER HEIGHTS

Frank Clune, the prolific writer of popular books based largely on Australian history, lived most of his life in Princes Avenue, Watsons Bay, just a few streets west of the Macquarie Lighthouse.

He claimed in his book, *Saga of Sydney*, that 'the best view of Sydney is from my verandah because I can see it all at once ... but probably several thousand others with a harbour view think that their views are the best'.

What he is referring to here is the Sydney obsession with harbour views, a mania that makes people work all their lives for a veranda that they have no time to enjoy.

If you want to see a view that Sydney real estate agents would value at a couple of million (you, of course, get to enjoy it free) the place to go is the Dudley Page Reserve in Dover Heights.

This is every Sydney postcard pasted together and come to life—the Harbour Bridge, the Opera House, the ferries on the harbour, the city skyline, as if arranged by some advertising art director for a tourism poster. If the view seems familiar, it's because countless television commercials have been filmed here.

Sorry, Frank, but this is the best view of Sydney, which explains why there is usually a small crowd of admirers up here in summer. Some bring along beach chairs and an esky. As the sun sets over the harbour, this is about the best show in town.

The Dudley Page Reserve is between Military Road, Lancaster Road and Portland Street in Dover Heights. Best viewing time—sunset.

BONSAI KORESHOFF NURSERY, CASTLE HILL

Australia's oldest bonsai nursery is run by Dorothy Koreshoff and her daughter Deborah, whose book on the art, science, history and philosophy of bonsai is considered a world classic.

Dorothy's late husband, Vitaliy Koreshoff, was born in Manchuria. As a boy, he learnt the art of bonsai from an old Chinese gardener. After arriving in Australia in 1928, Vitaliy was possibly the first person to start growing bonsai here. His private collection can be inspected at the nursery, along with trees developed by Dorothy and Deborah.

The oldest tree in the nursery is the cedar which Vitaliy started training into a semi-cascade style in 1930. It may be an infant compared to some of the thousand-year-old Japanese and Chinese specimens, but this is almost certainly the oldest Australian-born bonsai. 'It's two months older than I am,' Dorothy Koreshoff says proudly.

There is also a wonderful display of *mame* or 'baby' bonsai, in pots small enough to balance on one finger. These miniature specimens include Port Jackson fig trees. Despite being among the largest trees in real life (you can see megalithic examples at Sydney's Royal Botanic Gardens), they are happy to be confined to a pot the size of a walnut.

As small as these are, they are giants compared to the ones grown by local baby bonsai specialist Doug Burges. In the early 1970s, he had a fig tree that was three quarters of an inch high and had thirty-six leaves. It had to be pruned with tweezers using a magnifying glass.

The Koreshoffs have a selection of other Australian natives grown as bonsai. Examples of Aussie bonsai include lilly pilly, callistemon, casuarina, banksia and a Queensland leopard tree. Some of these are over fifty years old.

Trees in the private collections are not for sale, but there are plenty to buy if you want. Bonsai can not easily be taken overseas but it is possible for an interstate visitor to take home a unique and lasting reminder of Sydney for around $20.

A Port Jackson fig bonsai will grow in most parts of Australia except Tasmania and will enable you, in the words of William Blake, to 'hold infinity in the palm of your hand, and eternity in an hour'.

The Bonsai Koreshoff Nursery is at Lot G, Telfer Road, Castle Hill. The nursery is signposted from Old Northern Road. The nearest major intersection is at Castle Hill Road.

CAR (NO LONGER) UP THE TREE, PARRAMATTA ROAD

One of the problems with writing a book about a fast-changing city like Sydney is that even its best-loved landmarks can disappear overnight. This then is a story of the car that is no longer up the tree, but should be. Who knows, if enough people complain, maybe they'll put it back.

For over thirty years a yellow Austin 7 Ruby, looking as if had been crashed there by Noddy while tipsy, was stuck halfway up a fig tree in a car yard on Parramatta Road, Ashfield.

Suddenly, one morning at the end of May 1998, it was gone. When new, non-automotive tenants took over the site, they decided to remove the vehicle, selling it to a classic car enthusiast who planned to restore it.

Taking an old, rusted car out of a tree seems like a fairly easy task. Not so. The car had obviously touched a cultural nerve. For the next few weeks, *The Sydney Morning Herald's* 'Column 8' was flooded with readers' fond memories of the car, revealing the mystery of how it, and two predecessors, had become tree-borne.

Cos Gory, of Drummoyne, revealed that he had bought the car in 1967 from the farm near Taralga where it had been sitting for fifteen years with a broken axle. He paid the farmer $10, then sold it a year later to what was then known as Apex Motors for $130. The Freestone family, owners of Apex Motors, revealed that they had removed the motor and tied the body halfway up the tree with steel cable as a promotional gimmick. A very successful gimmick —the car became an icon.

But locals remember an even earlier car up the tree. Further reports to the *Herald* suggested that this is the site of the first car yard in what is now twenty solid kilometres of pre-loved automotive bargains.

Around 1910, according to a *Herald* reader with an amazing memory, Norman L. Agate started a Peugeot agency on this location, and it was he who first had the inspiration to fix a Peugeot Bebe up a tree. The Peugeot was later updated to an Austin Big 7, according to Barry Lake, who used to work across the road, at the sports car yard run by motorsports legend Leo Geoghegan.

Several other readers sent in eyewitness accounts of cars up the tree before the most recent Austin 7.

So what does this prove? If nothing else, it shows that people have unexpected fondness for life's little pleasures, even if we only really notice them once they are gone.

Fortunately, and purely by coincidence, I decided to stop and take a photo of the car a week before it was removed. If they ever decide to put it back (by popular demand), I can show them exactly where it was.

The car is gone but the tree remains at 542 Parramatta Road, Ashfield.

CASA CLAVEL, BELLEVUE HILL

The extravagant Moorish style mansion in Drumalbyn Road, Bellevue Hill, has been modernised by its most recent owner, eliminating most of its original eccentricity and removing its original name, Casa Clavel.

But you can't cover notoriety with a coat of paint, and this historic home still retains much of the atmosphere of its colourful past.

This house originally belonged to Dr Reginald Stuart-Jones, one of Sydney's most flamboyant medicos. Even more flamboyant, possibly, than Dr Edelsten. A successful Macquarie Street gynaecologist, Stuart-Jones also enjoyed the darker side of life. He was variously involved in abortion rackets, sly grog operations and the running of illegal casinos. With a well-deserved reputation as a punter and a playboy, the wild parties held at Drumalbyn Road were legendary.

Like several self-made men before and since, this doctor got his kicks from mixing with the underworld. Sometimes he got too close for comfort. Around midnight on October 31 1944, two small-time crims turned up at Casa Clavel and asked Stuart-Jones to check out a sick mate in their car. Just like in the movies, it was a trick. Stuart-Jones found himself in the back of the car with a gun aimed at his head. He was escorted to the edge of the cliffs at Maroubra and told to say his prayers.

A shot was fired. The bullet passed right through his body, perforating a lung in its travels. But somehow the doctor was still very much alive. The hitmen were so shocked they eventually dropped him off at a private hospital in Randwick.

Such were the daily goings-on at Casa Clavel.

At the sensational trial into Stuart-Jones's attempted murder, juicy details filled Sydney's scandal sheets for weeks.

'The trial was almost a fiesta for Sydney's underworld,' reported the *Truth* newspaper, 'Each day they arrived in cars. On one occasion, nine handsome limousines parked outside the court were owned, according to a detective, by reputed gunmen.'

Evidence linked the doctor with king crims like 'Chow' Hayes, Donald 'The Duck' Day and Richard Reilly. Tales were told of the doctor smuggling black market booze and drugs to American soldiers in his luxury yacht. The sordid details of the tangled affairs of Stuart-Jones's considerably younger wife Mary Kathleen were made public. She too, obviously, liked to mix intimately with the underworld.

Stuart-Jones built Casa Clavel in the early 1940s. Despite war restrictions, no expense was spared. In its original form it featured five bedrooms, three bathrooms, a curved balcony overlooking the harbour and a garage spacious enough for a couple of the doctor's imported American limousines.

Inside the house were not one but two grand pianos, a billiards table and, in the basement, a private shooting gallery. Stuart-Jones made a habit of never leaving home without his revolver.

It was a swell party while it lasted. In 1947, Stuart-Jones was forced to sell the house to pay off a considerable amount of back taxes he had forgotten to pay. Soon after, he divorced Mary Kathleen and married an even younger, even blonder model. They made an interesting couple. Stuart-Jones liked to wear loud Hawaiian-style shirts cut from the same cloth as his wife's dresses.

Since its most colourful period, Casa Clavel has changed hands several times but, despite all attempts to make it look more respectable, to me it will always remain the house that Dr Stuart-Jones built.

The doctor died of a heart attack in 1961.

Casa Clavel is at 61 Drumalbyn Road, Bellevue Hill. Please note this is a private residence.

STREET OF A HUNDRED HORSES, CONDELL PARK

At first sight, Ellis Street in Condell Park appears to be like any other road in the western suburbs. The first indication that something special happens here is the warning sign on the corner of Yanderra Street. The sign has the silhouette of a horse. To be accurate, it should have the silhouette of a horse and sulky. Ellis Street is Sydney's residential centre of harness racing. If you drive along, you will notice that just about every house has a horse float parked out front, and down every driveway, bar one or two, there are stables in the backyard. If you live in Ellis Street, it appears to be compulsory to own a pacer (as trotters are officially called these days).

Going to the trots was a big thing in the 1950s, even inspiring a neat piece of Aussie rhyming slang, 'the red hots'. Horses like Paleface Adios (The Temora Tornado) were as well-known as their more illustrious cousins, the thoroughbreds.

Today, harness racing is a minority sport, but for horse lovers who can't afford a thoroughbred, it still has a big appeal. It appears most of those remaining enthusiasts choose to live in this one street.

In Ellis Street, the big action happens at the crack of dawn, when every man, woman, dog and horse emerge from their houses and head off to do some laps of the nearby Bankstown Paceway.

No need to load the horse in the trailer, just hitch up the sulky and hit the road. Most mornings it's an equine traffic jam.

There are other streets in the area that have a horse or two, but for some reason, nothing matches the saturation level of Ellis Street.

For those who aren't interested in horses, but have a rose garden, there's another very good reason to pay a visit to Ellis Street. Most of the houses have signs out front offering bags of manure. There's an unlimited amount—and it's free.

Ellis Street, Condell Park, is close to Bankstown Paceway.

LITTLE BITS OF EGYPT, CROWS NEST AND KU-RING-GAI CHASE

It's a little known fact that you can see two of the wonders of ancient Egypt right here, avoiding expensive airfares, life-threatening airline food and the inconvenience of having to deal with foreigners.

The Crows Nest Pyramid which is close to the McLaren Street entrance of St Thomas Cemetery, may be considerably smaller than the ones at Cheops, but it's much more modern. Erected circa 1845 by local identity Alexander Berry as a memorial to his wife, it's not known whether she was mummified before being placed inside.

Sydney also has its very own sphinx, in Ku-ring-gai Chase National Park (first turn right after entering from Bobbin Head Road), a great deal closer than Egypt.

Private W. T. Shirley, a World War I veteran, carved the eighth-scale sphinx during the years 1925 and 1926 from a solid block of sandstone. He was recovering from war injuries at the time. This is his personal tribute to his fallen comrades.

It may be smaller than the original, but in one sense it's an improvement. Possibly because he was 'severely gassed during the war' (according to the plaque), Shirley chipped onto his sphinx an enigmatic smile, giving it a facial expression somewhere between Mona Lisa and Mickey Mouse.

The sphinx has recently been renovated and the beautiful bush surroundings are being landscaped.

The Crows Nest Pyramid is in St Thomas Cemetery, McLaren Street entrance. The Ku-ring-gai Sphinx is near the Bobbin Head Road entrance to Ku-ring-gai Chase National Park.

THE GROTTO CAPRI RESTAURANT, KENSINGTON

A seafood restaurant called the Capri has existed on this site in Kensington since 1951, but in the early 1960s, the Battista family took over in more ways than one. Inspired by the famous Blue Grotto near Capri, on the Italian Riviera, they decided to turn the restaurant into a replica of an underwater cavern.

Over the years things have got a little out of hand. The original room has been joined by another two, which have also been turned into grottoes. Now there is a total seating capacity of 200. The exterior has also been decorated grotto-style.

If you're interested, book a table and ask to see one of the original 1960s menus, which tells the full story in detail. In 1960s measures, they used ten tons of steel, three tons of plaster, one ton of cement and five tons of Italian marble to create the grotto effect, along with countless real or imitation lobsters, turtles and shells.

Three 10hp pumps are used to create the 'trickling sounds of blue fresh flowing waters'. These constant trickling sounds may inspire you to visit the toilets once or twice throughout your meal, but this is a pleasurable experience in itself. The male toilets feature pale blue fittings. The female powder room, so I'm reliably informed, is done up in shell pink.

Some may call it kitsch, but to me the atmosphere is magical. On my last visit, the background music was a tape by Perez Prado which included the music from the movie *La Dolce Vita*. You could almost imagine Anita Ekberg dancing in the fountain in a black dress. Fellini would have loved this place, as did the producers of the ABC television series, 'Wildside'.

The Grotto Capri Restaurant is at Nos. 97–101 Anzac Parade, Kensington. Open Tuesday to Sunday. Phone 02 9662 7111 for bookings.

JOE FERLA'S MAD MONSTER GARDEN, SUMMER HILL

Down a quiet back street in Summer Hill, a suburb in Sydney's inner west, hides a garden full of wild animals. Over the last twenty-five years, Guiseppe—'call me Joe'—Ferla has sculpted dozens of wonderful animal shapes from shrubs.

His spectacular topiary garden ranks with the best in Australia, the more so because his art has an added childlike quality. Joe likes to fashion details like eyes, tongues and beaks out of painted metal or wood which give his creatures a cartoon dimension.

They're fun. His Tony Lockett-sized gorilla holds a banana, his kangaroo has a joey in its pouch, and his snake has a forked tongue. The most popular with local kids is the huge green dinosaur sprawling across the front of the house.

Most of Joe Ferla's works of art can be enjoyed from the footpath, especially the neat rows of chickens which line the pathway to the front door. Down the driveway, a replica of the Sydney Harbour Bridge appears to be going well, while unseen in the backyard are a few more bears and gorillas.

Joe Ferla's topiary garden is at No. 51 Henson Street, Summer Hill. This is a private residence, so no trespassing please, but Joe Ferla is a friendly man who may well show you around if you catch him clipping away in the front yard.

SUSPENSION BRIDGE, NORTHBRIDGE

As sacrilegious as it may sound, there is a far more interesting bridge in Sydney than the big one spanning the harbour. Northbridge Suspension Bridge, crossing Tunks Creek and connecting the blue chip suburbs of Northbridge and Cammeray, is not only a folly in the architectural sense, it was also a major financial flop. Complete with Gothic turrets, castle battlements and, according to the original design, space for 112 mock cannons, the bridge is little more than a very expensive publicity gimmick for a new housing estate.

In 1891, the North Sydney Tramway and Investment Company, a group of land developers, built the bridge as a means, they hoped, of enticing thousands of homebuyers to cross over and buy housing blocks. It was by any standards a huge gamble. They invested £100,000 (add a couple of zeros for today's dollar equivalent) on what was basically an access road, banking on plans that a tramway would be built linking the city with their new suburb.

This didn't happen for another twenty years. By that time, the public had stayed away and the company had collapsed. Not so the bridge. This spectacular structure was taken over by the State government in 1912 and survives as a reminder of its long-forgotten but over-ambitious creators.

I wonder how many of the commuters who use the bridge every day realise that this is a really a monument to poor financial planning. They're probably too busy worrying about their own rising debt levels to care.

Although it is still called a suspension bridge, even on street directories, the steel cables holding the twin castles together were replaced in 1936 by an arch and girders. As bizarre as it may look from road level, the best way to appreciate this folly is from below. Way, way below.

You can do this by taking either The Boulevard (south of the bridge) or Cliff Avenue (north of the bridge) and walking downhill until you enter Tunks Park. The deep ravine that the bridge originally spanned has since been levelled and turned into lush sports fields, so it is a relatively easy walk to get a fish-eye view of the bridge. It's worth the trip. From down here, especially on misty days, it has a spooky, fairytale quality.

Northbridge appears to have inspired a minor castle revival in the northern suburbs of Sydney. Apart from Castlecrag, an entire suburb based on a medieval theme, there is another quirky castle-like structure on the hill just above the bridge's southern turrets. If you turn off Miller Street into Pine Street, Cammeray, you will see it at the very end of Bellevue Street. It's not really a castle. It's an electric light substation, built in 1915.

Northbridge Suspension Bridge can be approached from the south by Miller Street, Cammeray, or from the north by Strathallen Avenue, Northbridge.

PLAZA IBEROAMERICANA, CENTRAL STATION

In a tiny park near the Surry Hills end of Central Station's Devonshire Tunnel, one of Sydney's lesser known sculpture galleries can be found.

The Plaza Iberoamericana celebrates the contribution of Spanish and Portuguese people to Australian culture. Opened in 1989, it features statues, in brass and stone, of prominent figures from Latin American history.

Here, for example, you can find out about the man who was indirectly responsible for naming our country. The Portuguese explorer Pedro Fernando de Quiros (1565–1615) gave the name Australia Del Espiritu Santo to the then unclaimed (by non-Aboriginals) southern continent.

Others in Plaza Iberoamericana have more tenuous connections to Australia, but are interesting in other respects. Where else can you see likenesses of General Don Bernado O'Higgins, the liberator of Chile, or Dr Jose Protacio Rizal, the national hero of the Philippines? Imelda Marcos, one of the few Latin American leaders to have actually visited Australia (for the opening of the Opera House) is conspicuous by her absence. Also featured is Jose Marti, described as a Cuban teacher and as a journalist, poet and politician who died fighting for Cuban independence in 1895.

The Plaza was funded by a number of Latin American individuals, social groups and companies. Al Grassby, the very colourful former immigration minister with the Whitlam government, was the president of the committee which helped set up the project.

While a pleasant way to catch up on your Latin American history, the park appears to be sparingly visited, except by the homeless. Perhaps this has something to do with its unexpected location, shoehorned next to the easternmost platforms of Central Station.

The Plaza Iboamericana is opposite 36 Chalmers Street, Surry Hills.

PROSPECT RESERVOIR

When you turn on a tap in Sydney, where does the water come from? Chances are it comes from Prospect Reservoir in the mid-western suburbs. Despite covering 512 hectares and being situated close to the major highway heading west, Sydney's main city dam goes largely unnoticed. Even long-term residents are unaware of its exact location, including news crews. When the 1998 water virus scare hit Sydney, and the filtration works at Prospect were blamed, some television networks showed file footage of Warragamba Dam instead.

It may be forgotten now, but Prospect Reservoir was once headline news. When it was completed in 1883, it was the largest dam in Australia with a capacity of eleven million gallons.

There are now much larger dams (like Warragamba) just outside the city limits, so Prospect is used primarily as a storage tank. But it is still from this place that water is directly fed to the city via pumping stations at Waterloo and Crown streets, and from there into your kitchen sink.

When you visit Prospect, it's fascinating to consider how such a large project could have been completed before the advent of petrol-driven earth-moving equipment.

A clue is provided in front of the jetty that leads to the old pump house. Here lies Pincott's Roller, a medieval-looking device carved from solid chunks of volcanic stone. This was used to pack down the dirt surface of the dam walls, in the same way that much smaller rollers are used to smooth cricket pitches.

Pincott's Roller was pulled by a team of bullocks. The roller must have been a valued piece of engineering equipment—it was dragged to this site all the way from Victoria by a team of ten (very tired) horses.

Despite the reliance on what we now consider primitive equipment, this project was completed in only five years.

Those who care less about the finer details of where their tap water comes from may still be interested in visiting Prospect. It has a secondary role as a pleasant oasis in the heart of the western suburbs. A road lined by stately hoop pines leads visitors to the shore of the lake or the lookout on the adjacent hill. It's hard to believe that you are smack in the middle of Sydney's suburban sprawl.

Prospect Reservoir is a popular picnic spot, one of the few opportunities in the west to relax by the water. There are barbeque facilities but swimming is not allowed. Also banned are boating, fishing, rollerblading and, according to the sign, the use of firearms. After the water pollution scare of 1998, they might as well add the dumping of dead animals to the list.

The entrance to Prospect Resevoir is on Resevoir Road, Prospect, and is signposted from the Great Western Highway. There is no admission fee.

ROLF HARRIS COOLIBAH TREE (AND OTHER MYSTERIES), ROYAL BOTANIC GARDENS

There was a time when the most-asked question at the Botanic Gardens Visitors Centre (usually in an American accent) was, 'Hey, where's your coolibah tree?' Until 1985, the embarrassing answer was, 'Sorry, we don't have one.'

This revelation is included in Edmund Wilson's 1992 book on the history of the Gardens, *The Wishing Tree* (Kangaroo Press, available at the Gardens bookshop). Wilson was a volunteer guide at the time, and the number of enquiries about the coolibah convinced him to initiate the planting of the tree most famously mentioned in Banjo Patterson's song 'Waltzing Matilda'. Strangely, no one had thought of planting one before. Wilson organised some seeds to be sent from Collarenibri in western

New South Wales and this botanical oversight was remedied in Heritage Week of 1985.

Australian folk hero Rolf Harris was invited to officially plant the tree, although a publicity-hungry politician named Laurie Brereton also had his hand on the spade. A high school choir sang 'Waltzing Matilda'.

The coolibah (*Eucalyptus coolabah*) likes to have its roots wet, especially in a billabong, so it was planted on the banks of the larger of the twin ponds in the Lower Garden section (maps available form the Visitors Centre). It has already developed a noticeable slant, weeping over the water.

Despite being planted by the entertainer most famous for having an extra leg (sorry), the Rolf Harris coolibah has just the one trunk at this stage.

There are countless other hidden treasures in the gardens, but two have especially fascinating histories. The mulberry tree on Lawn 17 has long been called 'the Shakespeare mulberry' because, according to legend, it is a direct descendant of the one Shakespeare planted in his back garden at Stratford-upon-Avon. 'That claim is now "iffy",' suggests Wilson, who has done some serious academic research on this matter. 'It could be a ring-in,' he warns.

At one stage he was even considering conducting a DNA test, comparing the genetic 'fingerprint' of the tree in the garden with that of a chair in the possession of the State Library. This chair was made from wood collected from the original Shakespearean mulberry when it was cut down.

Edmund Wilson's suspicions were aroused when leaves from another tree believed to be a direct descendant proved to be a separate species to the one on Lawn 17. The jury may be out on the tree's credentials but, imposter or not, it's a nice tree.

Another of life's little mysteries lies close to the smaller of the two entrance gates near the Opera House.

Here stands a statue known as 'The Satyr', hiding in a Lord Howe wedding lily bush. It has long been suspected that the sculptor, Frank 'Guy' Lynch, modelled the satyr's face on that of his brother Joe, who had recently drowned after falling off a harbour ferry. According to legend, Joe Lynch, who was rarely sober, was dragged underwater because his coat pockets were filled with beer bottles. This is the same drowning man immortalised in Kenneth Slessor's famous 1939 poem, 'Five Bells':

'Where have you gone? The tide is over you,

The turn of midnight water's over you'

'The Satyr', bearing the impish face of Joe Lynch, stares out over the very spot where he fell to his death from the ferry. It's a wonderful story, but surely too good to be true? Edmund Wilson has also researched this matter, and he insists it is true.

The first example of a Wollemi Pine to be planted by human hands is in the Botanic Gardens, next to the 'I Wish' statue. This historic tree is unfortunately surrounded by a large cage, to protect it from human predators.

Entrances to Sydney's Royal Botanic Gardens are in Macquarie Street, Mrs Macquarie's Road and next to the Opera House. Open every day during daylight hours. There is no admission fee.

ROOKWOOD NECROPOLIS

This is the cemetery that has become part of the vernacular— as in 'How are you feeling today?' 'Terrible, crook as Rookwood.'

Rookwood Necropolis, to give this boneyard its correct Victorian title, is a source of many surprises. Established in 1867, it is the largest nineteenth century cemetery in the world, covering 315 hectares in an area just a kilometre or two from the Olympics site at Homebush.

Once thought of as a place to avoid, Rookwood has recently been rediscovered. Historic graveyards, and this one in particular, keep more than bodies. They also keep botanical secrets, as *Gardening Australia's* Mary Moody revealed recently on this television show.

Rookwood is a virtual timewarp, containing some of the rarest specimens of heritage roses in Australia. In spring, this cemetery explodes with flowers, but be warned, there are severe fines (up to $5,000) for picking any. The older sections are particularly rewarding. Some parts near the railway lines look as if they have only been visited by ghosts in the last fifty years.

Weeds proliferate, but a small team of gardeners and heritage enthusiasts are slowly restoring both the gravestones and the original plantings.

Magnolias and camellias can be seen among the lantana, some dating back to Victorian times.

The Heritage Rose Society is especially interested in Rookwood. They have found a damask-style rose growing here that is so rare it can't be positively identified. They refer to it as the Cemetery Rose. For those interested in the history of this cemetery, guided tours are held throughout the year. Tours of the older gravestones are especially fascinating. A particular favourite is the larger-than-life sandstone statue of Robert Hancock, who died in 1876. He is depicted wearing the tight breeches of the period, but when originally sculpted his pants were so body-hugging that a part of his anatomy had to be re-worked to avoid embarrassing the womenfolk.

Another feature of most tours is a visit to Frazer's Mausoleum in the Independent Section. This 'high Victorian Byzantine Gothic' masterpiece looks as if it has escaped from a horror movie. Built in 1894 at a cost of 5,000 pounds (around half a million dollars in today's currency), it is the largest monument in the cemetery.

A room in the historic 1925 Rookwood Crematorium on Memorial Avenue contains the only Museum of Funeral History in Australia. Believe it or not, this is fun. Here you can see displays of unusual caskets and urns from around the world, plus a photographic history of Rookwood's former Mortuary Station.

Decorated with herald angels like something out of a Cecil B. de Mille film set, this was the sister station to the one still standing in Regent Street, just down from Central Station. Special funeral trains used to run on this line, with mourners and clergy in the front carriages and the deceased riding in the rear. The train picked up passengers along the way at stations which carried a red flag.

Sadly, Rookwood's dead end to the mortuary line was dismantled stone by stone and has been rebuilt in suburban Canberra as a church.

As people begin to lose the notion that graveyards are spooky places, Rookwood is becoming a popular picnic venue. There are even barbeque facilities here and I'm not referring to the crematorium.

Entry to Rookwood Necropolis is in Rookwood Cemetery, Rookwood, from East Street. It is open during daylight hours. The Museum of Funeral History is open Monday to Friday from 9am to 5pm, and Saturdays and Sundays from 9am to 4pm. There is no admission fee. For information on guided tours, contact the Friends of Rookwood Society on 02 9499 2414.

SNAKE CHARMERS OF LA PEROUSE

A trip to the snake pit at La Perouse has been a Sunday tradition since the turn of the century. Professor Fred Fox was the first to show his collection of reptiles in the area.

Members of the Cann family began to demonstrate their snake-handling abilities in the 1920s. George Cann, who died in 1965, was the most legendary, partly because he claimed to have been injected with so much antivenene during his life that he was completely immune to snake bites. He worked during the week as curator of reptiles at Taronga Zoo.

Today, George Cann's sons, John and George Jnr, carry on the family tradition. They work alternate Sundays. The area has been called Cann Park in honour of the snake men.

This show is more an education than a circus, with a strong emphasis on respecting reptiles and safeguarding their natural environments. But snakes will be snakes and the sight of a deadly copperhead making a lunge is always a feature.

Lizards are also displayed, including the lace goanna, capable of inflicting a bite that requires twenty to thirty stitches. John Cann says that only one of his reptiles has ever escaped during a show. An eastern water dragon managed to jump the barrier, made a run for it, and was never seen again.

The La Perouse snake pit is a small grass enclosure overlooking Botany Bay near the end of Anzac Parade. George and John Cann's snake demonstrations run every Sunday and most public holidays, weather permitting. There is no admission fee, but donations are gladly accepted. Check with La Perouse Museum (phone 02 9311 3379) for further details.

Rooftop Wetlands, Surry Hills

You'll have to hire a helicopter to fully appreciate Sydney's most fascinating inner city garden. When businessman Max Frost decided to build a flat on top of the six-storey office block he owns in Surry Hills, he wondered what to do with the rest of the roof space.

His solution, a piece of lateral thinking worthy of Edward De Bono, was to flood it. This shallow layer of water not only helped cool the building but also allowed bullrushes and other wild grasses to grow. He then added large rocks to create a Japanese-style water garden. Soon birdlife began to gather in his unique sixth-storey wetlands. He has already had several species flying in to breed, although there is a slight technical problem to overcome. A few of the ducklings have been swept off the roof in storms.

Max Frost's flat forms an island in the centre of his lake but the water is shallow enough for him to go for walks if he wears gumboots. But the real joy is to sit on the balcony at sunset and watch the inner city wildlife.

The only sign from the street that this is an office block with a difference is the clump of wild grass leaning out over the footpath. You can see this if you look up from the opposite side of Holt Street. This is a private residence so, apart from the helicopter, the only way to see this unique environment is to look at a display of colour photos in the foyer.

The rooftop wetlands garden is on top of The Centre, Nos. 46–56 Holt Street, Surry Hills.

Tank Stream and other Underground Delights

A small stream winding down to Sydney Cove was the main reason why Sydney is situated where it is and not down amongst the swamps of Botany Bay. The Tank Stream (so called after the water was diverted into a series of storage tanks) was our first water supply. But as soon as white settlers built on its sandy banks, things started to go wrong.

By 1826, the water was already too polluted with sewage and rubbish to drink. By 1878, the Tank Stream was completely covered over to prevent disease. Today, few Sydneysiders even know where it is.

It's still there, but only just. These days, the Tank Stream is used mainly as a stormwater drain. Around the time of the 1988 Bicentennial celebrations, the Water Board arranged some public tours of the more accessible parts of the stream (or tunnel, as it now is). These tours began in Angel Place, just off George Street, where some of the original 1850s brickwork still exists. Upstream sections are too small for public access.

The tunnel continues downstream, running between George and Pitt Streets, until the original path had to be diverted around the foundations of the Australia Square Tower. The tunnel then passes under Bridge Street, so called because Sydney's first bridge was built here to cross the then open stream.

The underground tours ended at a convenient manhole in Crane Place, near Pitt Street, where a weir stops human progress. The flow of water is eventually discharged into the harbour at the western end of Circular Quay, but this exit is below the waterline.

If all this sounds exciting, almost romantic, consider this eyewitness account of a Tank Stream tour by Brian and Barbara Kennedy, as featured in *Subterranean Sydney*:

'Water Board hard hats and Water Board torches are handed out and then you put on a safety belt as you climb down the rungs of the manhole to the drain three metres below. The drain is low and slippery and your neck soon begins to ache from crouching as you slosh forward up to your ankles in water; it is then you begin to wonder why you came down this drain. The walls are alive with cockroaches. They seem to like it down here.'

Little wonder these public tours were discontinued. 'Too claustrophobic,' suggested a Water Board official when I made enquiries.

But if you have a passion for exploring the underworld, there's always the mystery tunnels at St James Station. When St James was built in 1926 as part of the current underground railway city loop, short additional tunnels were dug for possible future extensions. The extension at the Circular Quay end of St James was to become world famous. It was used by General

Douglas MacArthur as his secret Sydney headquarters during World War II. Another section of unused tunnel extends under Hyde Park.

You can see these secret tunnels by booking on an Australian Railway Historical Society guided tour. These are held on the third Saturday and Sunday of every month except December. You'll need to bring your own torch, old clothes and sturdy boots—some of the sections are ankle-deep in water.

Unfortunately, another thrilling underground tour of Sydney can only be enjoyed if you are lucky enough to be a maintenance engineer with the Metropolitan Water Sewerage and Drainage Board. Once a year, engineers (and close personal friends) travel down the main Bondi sewer in a fleet of canoes (yes, the obvious pun is intentional).

The Bondi sewer follows the course of Oxford Street, but a metre or two underneath. Occasionally this trip has been timed to coincide with the City to Surf Fun Run. The sewer team wins every time.

According to the intrepid paddlers, the smell isn't too bad once you get used to it. We'll have to take their word on that. 'People in bare feet or wearing thongs or sandals cannot be allowed to tour,' insists ARHS organiser Grahame Thurling,

Another unique Sydney underground experience can be much more easily experienced. What was once billed as 'the longest moving walkway in the southern hemisphere' takes pedestrians from the Domain Parking Station on Sir John Young Crescent to a choice of exits near St Mary's Cathedral and the Archibald Fountain. And vice versa, of course. There's no charge.

Built in 1961 but freshly renovated with zany murals, the Domain walkway is a handy shortcut for those walking into the city from the east. Unless I'm mistaken, the new, improved walkway moves at a faster pace than it used to, which makes me wonder what top speed an athlete like Cathy Freeman could reach on this device.

For details of tours of the tunnels at St James Station, contact Grahame Thurling on 02 9749 5820. Cost is $10 for adults and $5 for students.

SYDNEY PARK, ST PETERS

Sydney Park is one of the most significant examples of urban regeneration in the inner city area of Sydney. This vast area (larger than the Royal Botanic Gardens) was once the site of a brickworks, a tip and a variety of factory complexes.

Over the last two decades this industrial wasteland has been covered with countless tonnes of landfill and turned into parkland. It will take many years for the transformation to be complete, but already the thousands of trees, mostly natives, are starting to reach maturity.

A feature of the park's design is the creation of a series of large grass-covered mounds. Apparently the height of these hills will drop by as much as two metres as the landfill slowly settles over the years.

The most prominent of these man-made mountains is next to the four old brickworks chimneys which mark the north-western corner of the park. The view from the top is spectacular, providing 360-degree views over the city, inner west, airport and southern suburbs. The distinctive metal sculpture on top of this hill is 'The Trail' by Michael Snape, although the many layers of graffiti are more recent additions by unknown local painters.

Sydney Park is the site of an annual outdoor sculpture exhibition in August, with experimental works scattered throughout, but you can't help feeling that the star of the show is the park itself. What you are walking on is a large piece of landscape art.

There are other treasures hidden in and around the park.

One is on the wall of a terrace house at No. 669 Princes Highway, directly opposite those four brick chimneys. Here is a faded sign advertising B.F. Goodrich tyres. All that remains of the original work is the company logo, three yellow stars and an image of a tyre painted at the top of the building, as if floating in space. The tyre has a whitewall which probably dates it to the 1950s or earlier. Whatever, the floating tyre sign now has the surreal quality of a Magritte painting.

A kilometre south along the Princes Highway, on the corner of Canal Road, is another example of automotive surrealism. The Dynamo Auto Electrician's building is a rare survivor from the days when service stations actually tried to look different from each other. This one succeeded wonderfully with its extravagant Moorish styling.

The current owners have recently given the building a fresh coat of white paint. They are aware of its social import but, when trying to trace its history, were told the council records had been destroyed in a fire. Their research suggests the building dates back to before 1930 and that it was used as a petrol station until 1964 when the pumps were removed. It could well be the oldest surviving petrol station in Sydney.

Back to the park and back to nature. At the south-east corner of Sydney Park (a significant but pleasant stroll through the rolling landfill hills) lies a small area of man-made wetlands. This section, on the corner of Campbell and Euston Roads, is surrounded by factories but, despite the air pollution and the constant roar of trucks, surprising numbers of wildlife have decided to make their home here in the inner city. The lake is not much larger than a couple of tennis courts, but already ducks are breeding happily in the bullrushes at the back. The murky water is also home to a couple of very large carp.

This miniature oasis is a popular lunchtime spot for workers from the nearby industrial complexes and especially so for truckdrivers. There are few other green spaces in Sydney which have space for trucks to park.

Sydney Park is bounded by the Princes Highway, Mitchell, Euston, Campbell and Barwon Park roads.

TOM BASS SCULPTURE, CBD

On the corner of Hunter and Castlereagh Streets, in Sydney's CBD, is a unique work of public art. Created in 1963 by Australian sculptor Tom Bass, the free-form sculpture is indented in the side wall of what was then known as the P&O Building.

These days, most pass by without paying it any attention, but there was a time when this work of art had more than its fifteen minutes of fame. As you can see, the sculpture happens to be set into the wall at a similar height to the urinals in male toilets. It also features running water, as was pointed out on the cover of the February 1964 issue of *OZ* magazine, beneath a graphic photo of three Sydney teenagers using the sculpture for what appears to be its intended purpose.

'To alleviate the severe drabness of its sandstone facade,' explained the *OZ* editorial, 'sculptor Tom Bass has set an attractive bronze urinal in the wall for the convenience of passers-by. This is no ordinary urinal. It has a continual flushing system and basins handily set at different standing heights. There is a nominal charge, of course, but don't worry, there is no need to pay immediately. Just P&O.'

This issue of *OZ*, perhaps the most infamous in its brief history, was the one that caused charges of obscenity to be laid against its three young editors, Martin Sharp, Richard Neville and Richard Walsh.

While the trio claimed that their magazine was only ever intended as a work of satire, the judge at their trial decided that this photo would encourage an epidemic of public pissing in Hunter Street.

For this and other alleged acts of obscenity, two of the three editors (who appeared in court wearing their old school uniforms) were sentenced to six months' hard labour. Sharp only got four months. After a public outcry, these sentences were later overturned.

Regardless, it soon became obvious that many late night visitors to the city were indeed taking the directions on the cover literally and, for all I know, still are. To look at the sculpture now is to wonder how anyone could have thought of it in any other way.

The Tom Bass sculpture is at No. 55 Hunter Street in the city.

UNIVERSITY OF SYDNEY

Unknown to most Sydneysiders, yet situated on the city's doorstep, the University of Sydney contains a number of hidden delights, including three small but fascinating museums that are open to the public and charge no admission. The Nicholson Museum (open Monday to Friday, 10am to 4.30pm) is located through the southern archway of the main quadrangle, close to the famous jacaranda tree, which is itself a museum piece.

Students have had a love–hate relationship with this tree and its predecessors ever since E. G. Waterhouse planted the first sapling on this spot in 1928. For unknown reasons, students tore out the first tree, which was promptly replaced by Waterhouse, a professor of German and a keen botanist. They also tore out the replacement and the one that replaced that one, until the professor outsmarted his foes by planting one that was simply too large to be removed with ease. Now 70 years old, it is expected to live another 30. This tree has become a Sydney icon, although today students dislike it for quite another reason. At the start of the summer, it explodes with purple flowers at the same time as the start of final exams.

But, back to Charles Nicholson and his museum. A qualified doctor, Nicholson was Chancellor of the University from 1854 to 1862, which enabled him to indulge his obsession for antiquities. His personal collection, one of the best in the world, was acquired through antique dealers and also from personal tours of Egypt. In 1860, he donated his collection to the university and here it has remained, being added to by new generations of Nicholson devotees. In 1966, the museum displays were modernised so that its full could be appreciated.

The space is divided into sections—Europe, Classical, Cyprus, the Near East and Egypt. The range of exhibits is amazing—from a 250,000-year-old flint hand axe to Roman copies of Greek sculpture, from Egyptian amulets to shards of Cypriot ceramics, made all the more remarkable by the fact that one man collected most of it.

Another extraordinary museum lies just a hundred metres away. The quickest route is through the Vice Chancellor's Quadrangle (also known as the Vice Squad), a small courtyard next to the Pharmacy building. This is another of the university's secrets. While many use it as a short cut, few, it appears, have time to stop and smell the flowers.

There are seats here where you can read or absorb the ambience created by Professor Wilkinson, a god-like figure among architectural students. He laid out this space with the help of the aforementioned Professor Waterhouse who, as well as being a lover of jacaranda trees, was a world authority on camellias. They are growing here in abundance, along with azaleas and clivias.

Hiding among the foliage are two sexy bronze statues, one of the god Mercury, the other of Fortuna. These were retrieved from the top of the old Hoadley's building on Broadway. A more recent sculpture, the 1989 horse by Shona Nunan, is in the south-eastern corner. Over the southern gateway is a memorial of the visit here, in 1920, by the then Prince of Wales, the man destined to become King Edward VIII.

The entrance to the Macleay Museum is almost directly opposite the Pharmacy building in Gosper Lane. This natural history museum has been gradually forced into the attic of the building, which was not what was intended when the museum was built in 1884. Alexander Macleay was Colonial Secretary of New South Wales but his true passion in life was the collecting of natural history specimens, especially butterflies. His mania at times left him on the verge of bankruptcy. When he died, he left his collection to his nephew, Sir William Macleay, who set up the museum.

Today, the Macleay Museum (open to the public Monday to Friday, 9am to 4pm) is like a giant curiosity cabinet. Prepare to be surprised. Between stuffed birds and preserved insects are such exotica as the fossilised faeces of what is thought to be a giant lizard or dinosaur, the skull of a one-eyed horse (on loan when I last visited) and a wooden fork used by the Fijian chieftain Thakambau to eat human flesh. Parts of a dodo skeleton are also featured. Here, too, is a dress worn by a Samoan woman in the 1880s, a display of vintage microscopes and, a more recent addition, one of the valve units from Silliac, the first computer to be installed in the university in the 1950s.

One feature of the collection was not available—a rare flask of Pasteur's broth. In search of this oddity, I was sent to the place that Rockefeller built. Behind the grandstand of the No. 2 Oval is the Blackburn building, erected in 1937 with funding from the Rockefeller Foundation. The main doorway features a bust of Louis Pasteur, so it is only fitting that his broth (see below) should be on loan to the Pathology Museum on the fifth floor.

This museum is intended mainly for use by medical students, although the curator, Glenn Holden, is happy to let in anyone who is genuinely interested in the history of medical research (phone 9351 2411 for details). He has also been running tours for school children, partly because he hopes the sight of a cancer-riddled lung may discourage teenage smoking.

This collection is definitely not for the squeamish. Here you can see, for example, the preserved heart of a man who was stabbed in a street fight in 1895. You can observe the effects of a gun shot on a vertebrae, or see how a small intestine looks after strangulation.

Natural diseases are also featured. A tonsil infected by gangrene and a brain afflicted with an intracerebral aneurism are just two of the hundreds of case studies, all neatly displayed in individual containers. Once you get over the initial shock that you are looking at bits of yourself, it becomes an enjoyable and educational experience.

However, it was the centre room that contained the treasure I was after. In 1888, the celebrated French chemist Louis Pasteur visited Australia to try and find a cure for the rabbit plague. He conducted experiments on Rodd Island using a special brew of beef broth. This is the only flask of that broth remaining in the world and for biologists it has much the same mystique as the Shroud of Turin.

The University of Sydney is in Camperdown, bounded by Parramatta, Missenden and City roads.

WESTMEAD CHILDREN'S HOSPITAL ART GALLERY

The first thing you notice is the waterfall. The fact that it's in the main foyer of a hospital is not the strangest part. What's really unusual is that this waterfall is trickling down a large chest of drawers.The Alice in Wonderland waterfall (its correct title is 'Drawers of Water', created in 1994 by the artist Jenny Turpin) is just one of many works of modern art placed strategically throughout the New Westmead Children's Hospital.

The idea of turning a hospital into a public art gallery was that of the now-retired chief executive officer, Dr John Yu, himself a dedicated lover of contemporary art. He commissioned curator Joanna Capon to assemble works of art that would appeal to both children and adults and help create a feeling of joy in what is traditionally a depressing environment.

Many of the works have an element of fantasy. Bruce Howard's 1992 surrealistic sculpture, *Galvanised and Corrugated Iron Bedstead*, is a prime example. The title says it all—it's a four poster bed made from metal and tin. It's quite beautiful.

While local artists are featured prominently, a highlight of the Outpatients area on Level 3 is a collection of photographs of the works of Christo, the Bulgarian artist best known in Sydney for wrapping, in the 1960s, a section of the cliffs near Maroubra. Christo is normally reluctant to have his work displayed anywhere except under his personal direction, so the Christo Wall is something of a coup.

The fact that the hospital is in the heart of Sydney's western suburbs means that some of the visitors to the hospital will be exposed to modern art for the first time. In fact, they may be sitting on it. A feature of the foyer is a work called *The Raft*, a series of beautifully moulded wooden shapes that are designed to be sat upon, although many visitors seem reluctant.

The reaction of the public to the works is fascinating to watch. Unlike exhibits in other art galleries, many of the works here are especially designed to be touched, even if social training tells us we shouldn't. The 'it's art, don't touch' mentality does not necessarily apply here.

Some of the best-loved pieces at Westmead were not strictly designed as works of art. Three of the original Luna Park mirrors, featuring curved glass to distort the image, are still as popular as ever with children. These were donated by Sydney businessman Leon Fink and have been placed in a kids' playroom.

The most interesting part of Dr Yu's artistic vision is in the way the works are integrated into the normal functions of the building. Paintings and sculpture are scattered throughout so that casual visitors are constantly surprised by what they see. Even one of the lifts—known by the staff as the Mondrian lift—has been artistically decorated.

Most of the hospital courtyards feature at least one sculpture. The largest outdoor area has been turned into a small-scale Chinese garden, complete with pagoda and water garden. This wonderful space was created from the remnants of the Chinese Gardens at Darling Harbour and in many ways resembles a miniature version of that place. It is delightful to stumble upon such an oasis in the middle of a very busy hospital complex.

The new Westmead Hospital is one of the true delights of western Sydney. The public are welcome to visit purely to see the artworks.

The New Children's Hospital is on Hawkesbury Road, Westmead. There is no admission fee.

WILLIAM WALL'S WHALE, AUSTRALIAN MUSEUM

Anyone visiting the Australian Museum in the city centre, will hardly fail to notice the magnificent skeleton of a giant sperm whale suspended from the ceiling. The question is, how did it get there?

This whale of a story (as researched by Steve Van Dyck, a curatorial officer with the Queensland Museum) is one of the most fascinating in the Australian Museum's chequered history.

On December 5 1849, the *Sydney Herald* newspaper announced that a large sperm whale, apparently dead from natural causes, had been found floating at sea and was currently being towed into Port Jackson. This was exciting news for William Wall, the curator of the Australian Museum, who had always wanted to have a sperm whale's skeleton on display. He negotiated with the owner of the ship who had claimed the whale's carcass and it was mutually agreed that, after the valuable blubber was removed, the remains would be donated to the museum.

Wall was now faced with the slight problem of delivery. Being a typically hot December, the whale was becoming increasingly fragrant. No one wanted anything to do with the rotting remains of a whale. Eventually Wall managed to persuade four Portuguese sailors who, for a considerable sum of money, agreed to flense the whale and treat the bones.

Unfortunately, they were busy for four days, so Wall was faced with finding somewhere to store the rapidly decomposing corpse.

The water police insisted it be taken from its temporary location at Neutral Bay after local residents complained of the stench. As Wall towed the whale to somewhere less populated, he noticed that a section of the tail, which contained important parts of the skeletal structure, was missing.

He began an extensive search for the missing tail section and after some time tracked it down (possibly by following his nose) to a wharf in Sussex Street. He rescued the putrid tail minutes before it was about to taken out into the harbour and sunk. He then began to tow the rest of the whale to Pinchgut (the island off Mrs Macquarie's Point, more formally known as Fort Denison), where, he hoped, it would remain quietly until the Portuguese whalers could start their work.

This was not the end of the drama. The head section of the now-disintegrating carcass soon came adrift and floated on the tide back to Neutral Bay, where it ended up in close proximity to the Collector of Customs' house. He immediately ordered the offensive morsel be towed back out into the harbour and disposed of.

By a strange coincidence, on board the boat towing the whale's head was Dr George Bennett, himself a former curator of the Australian Museum. Thinking it may be of some use to the museum, he had the foresight to secure the head to a rock, rather than let it disappear without trace. Wall, being told of the missing head, just managed to rescue it before the jaws were damaged by a voracious species of marine life known as 'small boys'.

Once the various sections of whale were assembled, the hugely unpleasant job of removing the putrefying flesh from the bones could begin. This took four days. The bones were then treated with lime and left to bleach in the sun. When this was done, Wall noticed to his horror that the skeleton was still incomplete. One flipper was missing.

Wall's astonishing good fortune continued. Hearing reports of a strange fish being found on the rocks at Woolloomooloo Bay, Wall investigated and discovered, to his joy, the missing flipper. His whale jigsaw was now complete. Once cleaned, the various pieces were carefully assembled and hung from the rafters, where the giant sperm whale skeleton (*Physter macrocephalus*) still welcomes visitors.

The Australian Museum is on the corner of William and College streets, Sydney. Open daily 9am–5pm; $5 adults, $3 concession, $2 children.

YARALLA AND THE THOMAS
WALKER HOSPITAL

T homas Walker, the president of the the Bank of New South Wales from
1869 to 1886, left an impressive legacy in the Concord area. Yaralla,
the family home he left to his sole heir, a daughter later to be known as
Dame Eadith Walker, is one example of his benevolence.

The Thomas Walker Convalescent Hospital (now Rivendell) is another
example of his generosity. He decreed in his will that it should be built,
'in the hope that many suffferers would be restored to health within it',
according to an inscription in the chapel.

Today, both residences, separated by Concord Hospital, are part of the
State health care system. But it is possible for the public to walk through the
grounds of both estates and imagine how splendid these places must have
been at the turn of the century.

For the adventurous, a walking track (well signposted but muddy in wet
weather) joins both the Walker properties, following the mangroves on the
banks of the Parramatta River. For those starting at Yaralla, the main
entrance is off Nullawarra Avenue, where a long driveway leads up to the
former home of Eadith Walker. This is now a dialysis unit for patients from
Concord Hospital. Several of the original buildings here are being restored,
including the stables. A flagged path leads down to the river and the
walkway to Thomas Walker Hospital. Access to this public walkway can
also be gained from the nearby Majors Bay Reserve.

The grounds at Yaralla are a faithful reproduction of an English country
estate. At times it is hard to believe you are in a suburb of Sydney not too
far from the CBD. The walking track takes you past paddocks where horses are agisted and past some virgin mangrove swamp, before winding
through the back parts of the Concord Hospital complex. Signposts make
this an easy enough maze to follow. The total distance is a kilometre and a
half, although the wildness of the terrain makes it seem longer.

A short flight of steps takes you into the Thomas Walker complex,
now known as Rivendell and a part of the Royal Prince Alfred Hospital. If
anything, Thomas Walker's hospital is even more spectacular than his

former home. It was designed by the architects Sulman and Power and completed in 1893. From the walkway, the first building to be seen is the grand water gate, a charming folly built over the water to welcome those arriving by boat and ferry. It has a domed turret and balconies on the upper floors. Sadly, it is now closed.

A short distance from the boat house is the Federation-style main building, which has to be seen to be believed. The two-storeyed central block has a tower with the roof supported by caryatids. Cherubs are featured on a frieze on either side of the tower. This angelic theme is continued inside.

While this is an operational medical centre, you may be allowed inside to see some of the architectural wonders and to walk past the marble bust of Thomas Walker to inspect the main hall, also called chapel.

The feature is seven stained-glass windows depicting a variety of Christian virtues. Inscribed on the walls is the aforementioned legend of Thomas Walker, and his family motto, *Per Varius Casius.* Walker was a believer in the John Wesley philosophy—make all you can, save all you can, give all you can.

The complex also features two inner courtyards in the Italian Renaissance style. The main drive from the building leads to a gatehouse where the Thomas Walker legend…'in the hope that many sufferers would be restored to health'…is again spelled out in sandstone letters.

As impressive as the tour of the Walker estates may be, I left with a slight feeling of disappointment. My quest to find the most secret part of the property had proved fruitless. There was no sign of Dame Eadith Walker's pet cemetery. According to a reference in a 1987 book, Dame Eadith buried her beloved dogs in a small graveyard at Yaralla. Each of her pets—Skye, Jock, Cooee, Dinkum and Little Woggie—had individual headstones. These markers were later moved to the Thomas Walker Hospital site but today are nowhere to be seen. The mystery was finally solved by checking with the Concord Heritage Society. I was told that the pet graveyard is now 'in storage' until a more suitable location is found.

Rivendell is part of the Concord Hospital Complex, Hospital Road, Concord, a 15 minute walk from Rhodes Railway Station. There are regular bus services to Concord Hospital from Strathfield Station or Ryde.

ODDS & ENDS

There are a number of minor attractions scattered throughout the suburbs of Sydney. Some may be worth stopping for, some may be worthy of a snapshot, others may just make you smile as you pass by.

STATUE OF BILLY, BALMORAL BEACH

In the park near the Bathers Pavilion is a charming tribute to Billy, a mongrel dog owned by Mosman street sweeper Cliff Williams. Billy accompanied Cliff on his rounds and was well loved by all who met him. The statue was erected in 1980. It's rare for mongrels to be honoured, so this is well worth a photo.

KFC, WOODVILLE ROAD, GUILDFORD

Back in 1968, this Kentucky Fried Chicken store was the first of its kind to be opened in Australia. As McDonald's didn't invade Australia until 1972, this may be the first fast food franchise in the country. You wouldn't know its significance as it looks, smells and tastes like any other KFC in the world.

GLENSYND MOTEL, RANDWICK

The motel at No. 35 Alison Road, next to Royal Randwick Racecourse, holds a unique place in Australian history. When the politician Donald McKay was assassinated in Griffith in 1977, drug baron Robert 'Aussie Bob' Trimbole was staying here. It was his solid-gold alibi at the Royal Commission into the death of McKay. However, the Glensynd got an undeserved reputation as the place where bad boys stay. Sorry, no Trimbole Memorial suite.

HORSLEY PARK GUN SHOP

Way out west, at No. 1848 The Horsley Drive, is Australia's (and the Southern Hemisphere's) largest gun shop. Even if you don't need a weapon (and you won't get one without a licence), check out owner Peter Abela's impressive collection of stuffed and mounted heads. Sometimes more than heads; a complete polar bear stands guard in one corner.

CAPTAIN COOK HOTEL, MOORE PARK

On the corner of Moore Park Road and Flinders Street, is the best of the many tributes to Captain James Cook in Australia. What better honour than to have a pub named after you? A large bust of the Captain graces the top of the building, overlooking one of the more chaotic intersections in Sydney.

ALAN BOND PLACE, MARSFIELD

In the hysteria following his 1983 America's Cup victory, Alan Bond and members of the winning *Australia II* team were honoured by having streets named after them in the Sydney suburb of Marsfield. Here, just off Epping Road, are Alan Bond Place, Ben Lexcen Place and John Bertrand Close. They may look like ordinary streets in an ordinary suburb, but now Alan Bond Place has another meaning. These days it's named after the man jailed for the biggest act of fraud in Australian history.

PARK AVENUE BRIDAL BOUTIQUE, PARRAMATTA

If Shop 306 in Westfield Shoppingtown at Parramatta looks familiar, it is. This is the one featured in the 1994 Australian movie, *Muriel's Wedding*.

MACQUARIE PLACE LOO

The highlight of the inaugural Sydney Open festival, run by the Historic Houses Trust in 1997, was a rare chance for women to visit an historic men's toilet. The circular dunny in Macquarie Reserve, with its glass domed roof, was built in 1908. Other Open Sydney tours opened the doors of the Opera House boardroom, the crypt of St Mary's Cathedral and a bank's safety deposit vault. For details on this year's Sydney Open, phone 1300 653 777.

WHALE BEACH ROCKPOOL

Sorry, but this is the best opportunity Sydney can offer to fans of Aussie soaps. Most of the outside scenes in *Home and Away* are filmed at Palm Beach and neighbouring Whale Beach. The rockpool at the southern end of Whale Beach is a regular location for the hunks and spunks to do their stuff, so you could be lucky.

MILPERRA PALMS, NO. 189 BEACONSFIELD ROAD, MILPERRA

When this western suburbs pub was known as the Viking Tavern, its car park was the scene of the famous Milperra Massacre on Father's Day, 1984. A dispute between two biker gangs, the Comancheros and the Banditos, resulted in seven dead and twenty-one injured. This is about the closest Australia has to a historic battlefield.

SHARON'S ANTIQUES, HABERFIELD

This fascinating shop at No. 49 Ramsay Street specialises in antique pedal cars. There are usually about twenty on display in the showroom and plenty more being lovingly restored in the back workroom. The market for these 'boys' toys' has skyrocketed in the last ten years, to the point where a fully restored Austin J40 is worth around $5,000. The main buyers are professional men trying, literally, to buy back their childhoods.

ALLAN MCQUEEN MEMORIAL

On the corner of Boomerang and Haig Streets in the city is a simple but moving memorial to Allan McQueen, a 26-year-old police constable who was shot on this spot in 1989 while trying to stop a car thief. Although Sydney is not a notably violent city, here is a stark reminder that over 200 police officers have died on duty since 1802.

THE DUKE'S SURFBOARD, FRESHWATER

Surfing's equivalent to the Shroud of Turin is the thirty-kilogram plank of sugar pine carved by Duke Kahanamoku from Hawaii. When he arrived in Australia in 1915 he was surprised to see that no one here was surfing, so he made this board to show locals how it was done. It hangs at the Freshwater Surf Club, just north of Manly.

NAT YOUNG'S WAVE, MONA VALE

Don't be surprised to see young blond-haired men genuflect as they pass the building on the corner of Pittwater Road and Mona Vale Road. This was once the surf shop owned by World Champion surfer Nat Young, a god-like figure among Sydney's surf cult. In 1980, when Nat opened his Fall

Line Surf and Ski shop at this location, he decided to paint a monster wave on the side wall to attract passing traffic. He asked a friend, Peter Stanton, to do the final artwork, but Nat and his wife Ti were very much involved in the design of the mural. According to his autobiography, they spent a week up on a scaffold 'cleaning the wall with sugar soap and painting on a base coat'. Nat sold the shop after a decade. The business is now part of the Surfection chain of stores, but fortunately they have decided to leave Nat's wave alone. It is still there—one of the landmarks of the Northern Beaches.

CHINESE MARKET GARDENS, ROCKDALE

It is an Australian tradition for Chinese to run market gardens, but few are now left in the suburbs of Sydney. There is one near Botany Cemetery, one near Bankstown Airport, and a large farm at Kyeemagh, just across the Cooks River from Mascot's East West runway. For over a century, several generations of Chinese have farmed these gardens, still wearing their traditional straw hats. Their shacks on Occupation Road are believed to have been here since the 1880s.

WAVERLEY CEMETERY TOURS

Midway between Bronte and Clovelly is the cemetery with the best views in Australia. Marion Corry, a Waverley librarian, has prepared some excellent themed guidebooks ($20 per copy from Waverley Library, Nos. 14–26 Ebley Street, Bondi Junction) to help you enjoy your private graveyard tour. *Who's Who Encore*, for example, lists dead theatricals. A personal favourite is the illustrated gravestone of Charles Peart, circus performer, who died while diving into a shallow tank of water. He missed.

INDEX